THAT'S COOL!

49 Awesome Tricks and Skills to Raise Your Cool Factor

By Ted & Tucker Baer

Warning & Disclaimer

Some of the tricks described in this book require balance, speed and hand-to-eye coordination. Readers should evaluate their skills before practicing or performing any trick and should avoid engaging in any activity that might be beyond their ability or comfort level. Some tricks may result in damage to property or injury to the participant or others if not done properly. Readers should review the instructions carefully to ensure that they have the skills necessary to practice and perform a trick, and should take all recommended precautions before practicing or performing any trick. Make sure there are no persons, pets or objects in the immediate area that might be injured or damaged.

Check with your physician to make sure you are healthy enough to practice and perform the skills described in this book.

Children should consult with a parent, teacher or other adult and have adult supervision before practicing or attempting to perform the tricks in this book.

The authors shall not be liable for any damages allegedly arising from the information in this book, and the authors specifically disclaim any liability from the application, use or misuse of any of the contents of this book.

To Moms. Try to find something cooler.

Table of Contents

INTRODUCTION

Have you ever walked by a piano in a public place and wished you could sit down and play, dazzling anyone within earshot? While we can't teach you how to play the piano, we can teach you forty-nine tricks that will dazzle anyone!

Throughout my life, I have been fascinated with "people" tricks - clever things that people do with objects in their daily lives. Each time I saw a good trick demonstrated, I was impressed. I also noticed that others around me shared my admiration. I was inspired to learn how to do each trick.

My background was also a factor in learning these tricks. My parents taught me to improve myself daily. They encouraged me to learn a second language, play a musical instrument, try different sports, sing, fix my own things, get an advanced degree, learn how to whistle, know how to cook. The skills you can accumulate in your life are endless.

I believe you should go through life with a bit of flair. Who wouldn't love to have the handy smoothness and panache of James Bond or have a day like Bill Murray's last day in the movie Ground Hog Day?

"Cool" can mean a lot of things. The word "cool" has more than twenty-five definitions in the dictionary, but the American slang usage of the word is quite unique and long lived. Used first in the 1930's, it still survives today.

People with money often give the impression of being cool because they own cool things, travel to exotic places or participate in elite activities. But money doesn't make you cool.

Cool is a mindset. It embraces being unique. Being cool has to do with being comfortable being you. You can always increase your cool factor. Be nice to people, be genuine, have principles, exude calmness, think before you speak, listen and be humble. Most importantly, be confident! Those things make you cool.

My sons, Tucker and Dillon, were quick to learn any trick I showed them. They also kept an eye out for anything new to bring home. You often found us all standing around trying to do a new trick. It was fun! We started making lists of these things and have put some of them into this book. They both helped greatly in the content of this book. Tucker joined me as a coauthor to help his old man out. Dillon and my wife, Lynnette, were our editors.

Our hope is that young and old alike will have fun and feel accomplished learning the tricks in this book while raising their cool factor! Learning a new trick is a great feeling. It improves your general confidence, your coordination, determination and patience. It will reassure you that effort produces good results. This is a great chance to raise your cool factor and impress your friends!

As an attempt to add humor throughout the book, I found the website punoftheday.com extremely helpful. I've taken it a pun myself to add many puns to the book. Kids and groanups can judge if they are laughtose intolerant, or not.

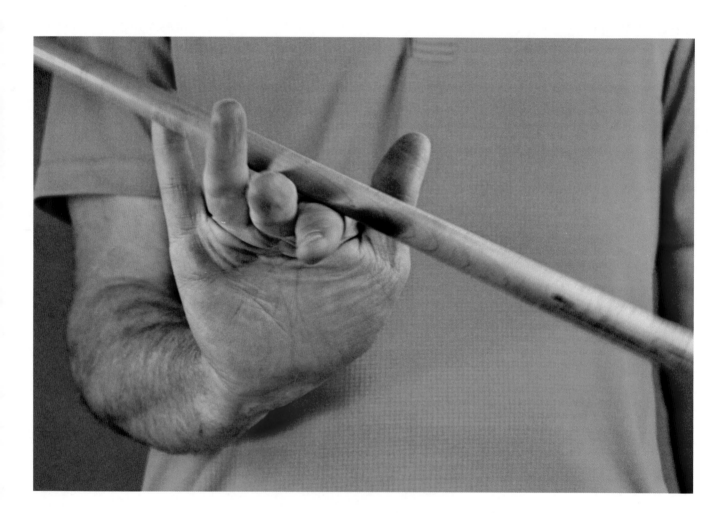

GENERAL ADVICE

The tricks in this book are generally easy to learn and guaranteed to impress anyone who sees them. They are not meant to be used in a demonstration, one right after each other, but rather casually integrated into your normal life. Do not overuse them. Just like a repeated magic trick will lose its appeal, so will these. When people see your trick, let them be impressed with your talents. Impress them further with being humble!

The book has a "start anywhere" format. Find a trick you are excited about, jump to the chapter and learn it. The tricks run the full gamut from being quite easy to difficult. Some will find certain tricks hard, while others find them easy.

With the easy tricks, you are apt to succeed after a handful of tries. Several tricks in the book are exceedingly difficult and may take a hundred tries to succeed the first time. Although it might only take a few seconds per try, many people will give up and deem the trick impossible. Those may become your favorite tricks. People who try to imitate you will fail without investing a lot of practice. For these harder tricks, realize that once you succeed in doing them the first time, the second success will come quicker. Hard tricks do get easier and easier with practice.

It is a fact that sometimes your fingers will cooperate, but you will often find that your thumb and forefinger are opposed!

Be sure to subscribe to THAT'S COOL on YouTube.

See our video on this book along with training videos covering many other cool skills. Visit our website at:
https://www.thatscool.cool

Both sites have links to recommended products.

#1 Go On Ahead

Question: For whom should you always remove your hat? The barber, for one. But there are other good reasons to remove your hat. In this chapter, you will learn to spin a baseball cap and acquire some slick ways of putting one on.

For all the tricks, pick a baseball cap that is stiffer or has a reinforced crown. Avoid caps or hats that are floppy. The hat needs to hold its shape.

To spin a baseball cap, hold it out in front of you, grasping the brim with your thumb, index finger and middle finger, and the brim pointing to the floor. Have the inside of the hat facing you, since you want your audience to see the more attractive side. Support the bottom edge of the brim up with the nail of your ring finger so that your hand stays out of the way of the spinning cap. Position your thumb facing you on the underside of the brim and have your index and middle fingers on the opposite side of the brim. The finger action you need is remarkably like snapping your fingers. The middle finger "snaps" to spin the hat around your thumb, rapidly spinning the hat on its vertical axis three hundred and sixty degrees. Expect this skill to take you a while to acquire. It must spin fast enough to not allow gravity to take over but not so fast that it launches out of your hand. As the hat comes around, develop the timing to grab it with your thumb and index finger. Done correctly, the brim of the hat should want to fall into the space between your thumb and index finger. As a beginner, it helps to lean the hat slightly away from you and to grab the brim slightly off center favoring the outside of the hat.

To make the trick look polished it is important to keep your hand as still as possible and stop the hat in the same position you start it in. This gives you the option of immediately repeating the spin. Alternatively, the trick can also be done using a lot of arm movement. Use a natural walking stride where you swing your arms. As you swing the arm holding the hat, spin the hat once and put it on. This might be done as you enter a room.

Like many of the tricks in the book, it may take you a few dozen tries to successfully perform this trick the first time, but fewer and fewer tries to become proficient.

There are several ways of putting on a baseball cap and they can be mastered more quickly than spinning the cap. For the first method, hold the cap with the brim facing you and with your four fingers on the top of the brim and your thumb supporting the hat from underneath the brim. Your elbow should be comfortably bent. Gently flip the hat toward you so that the top is resting on

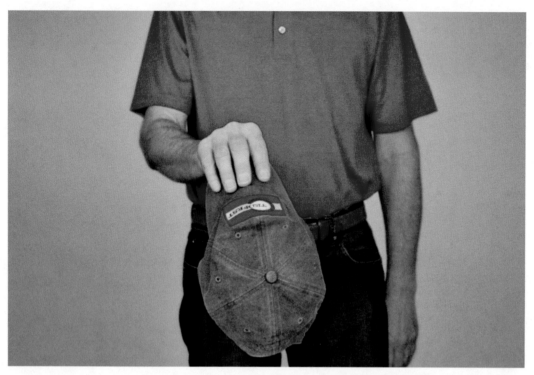

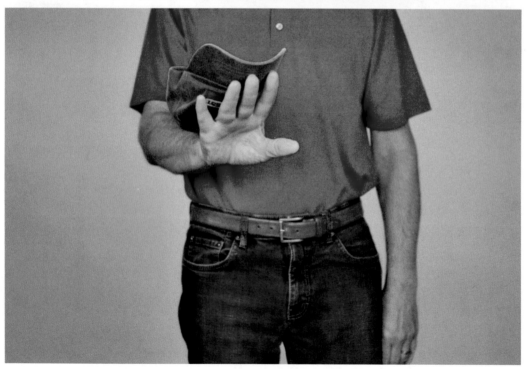

the back of your hand and wrist. Immediately, raise the back of your hand while balancing the cap and put it on your head pulling the brim down. Use your other hand to initially help you. Either leave the brim facing backward or dramatically rotate the brim around until the hat is facing the front. Practice in the mirror until you can do it without help from the other hand and the whole process looks smooth.

For the second method of putting on a baseball cap, hold the hat right side up with both hands. Have the brim facing you. Place your thumbs on the top of the cap at the point on

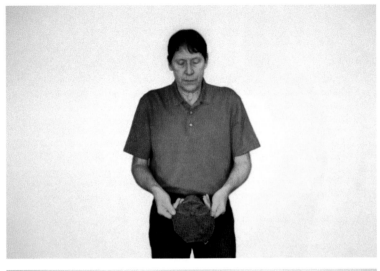

either side where the brim connects with the sides of the hat. Have your index fingers on the bottom side. Put your nails of your other fingers on the top of the brim. Start the cap down by your waist with the inside of the hat facing your body and the brim pointing up. Swing the brim of the hat out away from you as you raise your hands. Loosen your grip and allow the hat to swing between your index fingers for one rotation. Then, grab the hat with your thumbs, continuing the rotation, to complete the trick. The thumbs are on top of the brim at this point. The rotation should feel like the hat is tumbling toward you onto you head. The hat will revolve two times from start to finish as you pull it on to your head. As with the other method, either leave the brim facing backwards or rotate the brim around until the hat is facing front.

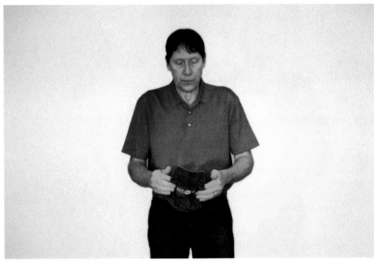

For the third method, start with the cap right side up and the brim facing away from you. This puts the hat on your head with the brim facing forward but is a little harder to master. In this situation, the cap will be harder to swing due to where the weight of the brim is. To balance it, you need to grab the brim with your index fingers pushed a little more toward the front of the brim. Have the rest of your fingers positioned with your nails on top of the hat, not the brim. Just like the other method, after the first rotation the thumbs continue the second rotation to complete the trick. If this is your preference, learning to do the trick the other way first will help you learn the general motion.

18

#2 The Straw Strip

At a fast food restaurant, most of us take a straw for our drinks. The straw is wrapped in paper for sanitation, but most people end up touching the straw in the process of putting it in their drink. The protection that paper offered against germs is lost. This trick allows you to put your straw into any drink without touching it. Feel free to help others as they will be impressed with your technique!

The trick is easy to learn. Grab a few paper-wrapped straws when you visit fast food restaurants so that you can practice it in private. Later when you demonstrate the trick, observers will admire it without having the time to acquire it. Grab the wrapped straw with your nondominant hand about

two inches from the top. Have your thumb pointing toward the short end of the straw. The straw should be supported by your middle finger, index finger and thumb. Use the first two fingers and the thumb of your dominant hand to grab the straw about a half an inch above the fingers and thumb holding the straw. Have your thumbs pointing toward each other. Pinch the straw with both hands and twist your hands in the opposite direction, breaking the straw's paper. The paper will break easier if you pull your hands slightly apart while doing this action. Continue to apply pressure with your dominant hand while you pull the paper off the long end of the straw. Be careful not to pinch the straw too hard as it can crack the straw, rendering it useless. Use the hand that is holding the paper-wrapped end to put the straw into the drink lid. Now that the plastic cover is holding the straw, pull off the remaining paper, leaving the straw in place. The hole in the plastic lid will provide enough resistance to allow you to slide the paper off.

If there is no plastic lid on the drink to support and hold the straw, advance your technique further. Instead of pulling the long end of the straw off first, start with the short end. After twisting, move a little slower pulling the short end of the paper stopping and pinching the straw right before you reach the end. Then pull the paper completely off the long end. Once you have placed the straw in the drink, remove the small end of the paper.

Since different companies manufacture different straws, you will find each brand varies as to how easily the paper will tear. With a little practice, you will be exstrawdinary!

#3 Credit Card Payoff

In our cashless society, we are constantly handing over our credit cards. This trick offers a fancier way to present it. You will flip the credit card off the edge of a table elegantly into the air, catch it between your fingers and turn it over as you hand it to someone. Later, you can practice with other items like a drink coaster, DVD, driver's license or any small item you come across that is flat.

The trick is an easy one to learn. Sit down at a table and extend the short side of a credit card off the table's edge. Hang about a third to a half of its length off the edge of the table. Keep the card square to the table's edge and have the card face up. Position your hand palm down, about two to three inches below the exposed edge of the credit card. Raise your forearm up quickly, using the back of

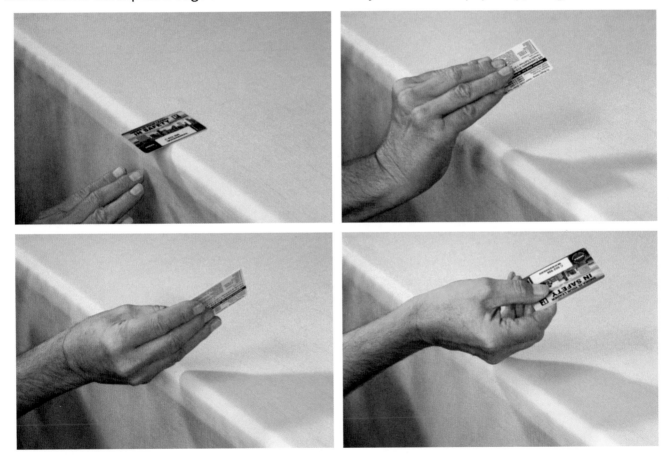

your fingertips to flip the card up off the table surface, rotating the card 180 degrees. The card will naturally drift away from you after you hit it, so make sure you follow it with your hand after you hit it in one smooth motion. Although your wrist naturally moves a bit, your forearm should be driving the movement. As the credit card flips quickly close your thumb and fingertips around it, catching the card. The back of the card should be facing up and your thumb should be facing down.

At this point, rotate your wrist so your hand is palm up and reach out to present the card. The credit card starts face up and ends face up when you present it. The beginning of the trick will be a blur by default, so slow the presentation portion down, making sure your viewers realize you did something special.

Once you have the trick down, practice it with other items. Also, practice the trick standing up using the edges of higher counters, furniture or ledges.

Make the trick look even better at restaurants. As you are flipping the credit card, have the check folder in your other hand and slip the card into it as you hand it to the server. Do not worry if no one pays attention, it is not a "glow bill" issue!

#4 Racquet Rotations

There are many different tricks that can be done with a tennis racquet. The four described below are easy to learn.

A tennis player is constantly picking up balls. In this trick, the ball is wedged between your foot and the racquet, popped up, bounced off the ground with your racquet strings and caught. It will save you time picking up the ball, save your back from bending over and it looks good!

Grab a tennis ball, a racquet and be wearing shoes. Any shoes will do. They do not have to be athletic shoes. Put the tennis ball down on any uncarpeted floor as you will need the tennis ball to bounce. Grab the tennis racquet as you normally would. Place the tennis ball so that it is near your instep or arch of the foot opposite the hand holding your tennis racquet. Place the face of your racquet next to the tennis ball, wedging it between the racquet and your shoe. Lift both your foot and the racquet simultaneously, pressing the ball into your foot with the racquet. The knee does not come straight up, but naturally swings a bit to the side or away from your body. Pop the tennis ball up into the air and use your racquet face to hit the ball down into the floor or court. Catch the ball as it bounces up.

To practice the rest of the tricks, find a grassy or carpeted area so that you can drop your tennis racquet without damaging it. Once you get these tricks down, there is little risk of dropping the racquet.

The Cradle Flip involves spinning your racquet just once. Grab the racquet where the strings meet the throat. Cradle the outside edge of the racket with all four of the fingers of your dominant hand, allowing your thumb to rest on the inside of the racquet's rim. The thumb's support will allow you to grip the racquet without much pressure. The head of the racquet should be pointing away from you. Swing the handle end of the racquet down and away from you while releasing your thumb's grip. Allow the racquet to spin 360 degrees around the back of your hand, ending with the handle landing in your palm. Notice that although your hand started up near the throat, the racquet's handle lands on your palm because the spun racquet has some momentum moving away from you. Once the racquet

lands, spin the handle so that your palm is now facing the ground. Having a loose grip will allow the handle to spin easily. The racquet should spin about one and a half rotations. This quick twist adds a little flash to a simple trick. Although it is easier to do the cradle flip away from you, the trick may be done parallel to your body, as well. Some may find this easier, especially with extended length racquets or if your arm length limits the racquet's clearance.

A variation on the Cradle Flip: as the racquet lands, instead of doing a quick spin of the handle, consider doing the 360 Flip. The 360 Flip simply involves launching the tennis racquet in the air so that it rotates 360 degrees before it is caught. To learn the trick, hold your racquet straight down along your side. Swing your arm and racquet out in front of you, and as you approach your waist level, release the racket to do a 360-degree flip and catch it by the handle. Once you get this down, add a twist of the handle as you release the tennis racquet to make the 360 Flip look better. With practice, you will learn to do the trick using your wrist instead of the long swing with a straight arm.

Lastly, learn to do the Twirl. Stick your index finger in the V-shaped area of the throat of the racquet and let the racquet go. The head will drop, and you will be in the starting position to swing the head away from your body. Spin the racquet fast enough around your finger to keep the finger in constant

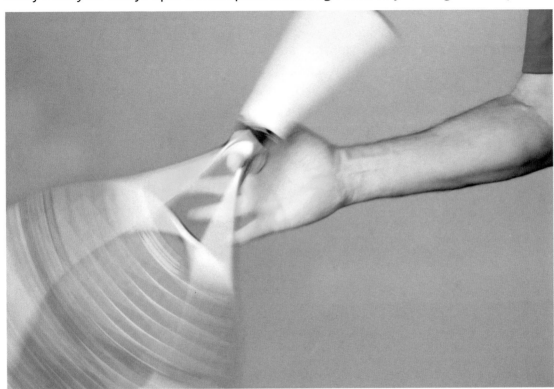

contact with the bottom of the V-shaped area. Keep the momentum up by making a little circle with your index finger. A slight curl on the index finger keeps the tennis racquet from flying off your finger. After a few twirls, wait until the racquet head passes by and close your hand, grabbing the handle. This is the part of the Twirl that will take some practice, as you need to feel the weight of the head swing by with your index finger to signal you to close your hand. Once you get the timing down, look elsewhere as you do the trick. That makes the feat even look better.

Between points, players often straighten out their racquet strings to concentrate or to just occupy time. It spin a long time, but now you have other options. The point is to not raise a racquet demonstrating your new skills, just let your gut feeling take over. Do not expect a smash hit, but maybe a volley of backhanded compliments. Anyway, the ball is in your court now!

#5 Quarter Master

This slick trick involves lining up quarters on your raised, bent arm then bringing your open hand down quickly, catching each quarter before it hits the floor. The hardest part of the trick is lining up the quarters without them slipping off.

To practice, put on a short-sleeved shirt, grab six quarters and stand over a bed. This will make it easier for you to retrieve the missed quarters and try again. Raise the elbow of your dominant arm until the elbow is pointed forward. The goal is to have your forearm fairly level to the ground. Have your open hand back by your ear with the palm facing up or preferably, toward your ear. Use your other hand to balance a quarter on the top of your forearm.

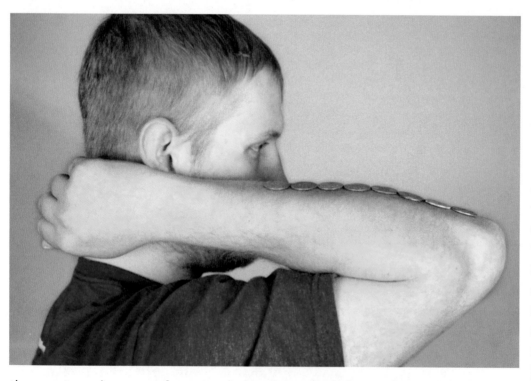

Quickly swing your hand forward toward the floor dropping your elbow quickly and grabbing the falling quarters. Once you can snatch one quarter consistently, try two, then three, etc. Six quarters is enough to dazzle people. Stacking the quarters is the easier method to learn. For a more difficult and more impressive presentation, line up the quarters along your forearm, then swing quickly forward to grab them. Lining them up will cause more attention from the crowd as people will be intrigued by what you are doing.

Once you have this trick down, it is easy to practice with other small objects that you find. Also, try the trick wearing a long-sleeved shirt. Now it is the time to let the whole world know how to handle change!

#6 Wrapped Around My Finger

Hibachi restaurant cooks dazzle their customers with intricate knife work and theatrics as they cook on steel grills in front of you. Most people enjoy the pretense that their cook is the descendant of a samurai warrior and find flying shrimp and onion volcanos truly memorable. Only trained professionals who practice daily should perform most of the tricks on display. Of the safer tricks they perform, spinning a spatula has minimal danger, but is quite impressive.

The secret to this trick is having a specially modified spatula: therefore, you will only be able to perform the spinning spatula trick when you have that modified spatula on hand. Although the trick will still require significant practice, it is essential to have the right equipment.

The spatula needs to have a wooden handle so that you can modify it. It also needs about a two-inch offset. An offset is the feature on the spatula that raises the handle above the blade so that turning the food on the grill is easier. The handle and the blade should be parallel, and the offset should bridge the two at approximately a forty-five-degree angle. The handle is normally about five inches in length. The metal blade should be around three inches wide and between five and eight inches long. It can be rounded or squared off on the end. The web site has a suggested spatula to buy.

Once you obtain the spatula, the bottom of the wooden handle, near the metal offset, needs to have a little bit of the handle cut off. Ideally, the gap between the wood handle and the metal offset should be the width of your index finger. Be conservative with your cut. If you cut off too little, you can always use a wood file to make it wider, if necessary. The cut should be at a slight angle away from the metal blade to make a notch for your finger. Use a file to make the angle greater if you think that will help you. Find someone to help you safely modify the spatula if you do not have the skills yourself.

Practice over a bed and protect any part of the bed's headboard or footboard with pillows. Guaranteed, the spatula will fly off your finger during practice sessions. Some spatulas have sharp edges that can damage your bedding or even cut you, so practice somewhere safe and be careful. You can also file the edges of the spatula or cover them with a layer of masking tape.

There are two ways to spin the spatula. The first way has some advantages finishing the spin. Learn the second way if you want to show off further.

In both methods, you use your dominant hand to hold the spatula with your index finger wedged in the notch you made. Use your thumb and pinch the spatula to secure it.

In the first method, the spatula is held horizontally upside down, with your index finger in the notch on the handle and your thumb supporting the spatula underneath. Have the handle pointing to the outside. To start the spin, twist your wrist, sending the handle downward while releasing your thumb. The spatula will spin clockwise for the right-handed and counterclockwise for the left-handed. Move your finger in a horizontal oval rather than a circle.

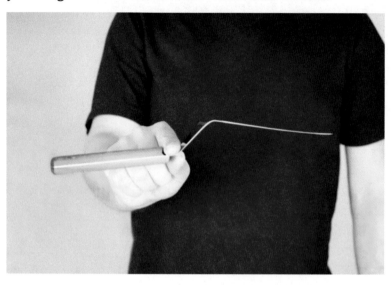

In both methods, during the spinning process you will feel when your finger has greater pressure against the handle. That is the time to exert energy to keep the spatula spinning. As you move your finger in a horizontal oval, it will accelerate as it is moves downward on the side of the oval. Your finger then slows down slightly until the next downward motion.

Spin the spatula until you feel that you are losing good contact and control, then grab the handle. You will find that you can handily grab the handle in this method, whereas the second method will require a little bit more practice.

In the second method, balance the spatula on your index finger handle up, blade down, finger pointing away from you and your thumb lightly placed at the base of the handle. Start the spin by twisting your wrist and releasing your thumb, taking advantage of the swing weight of the metal blade. The spatula will spin counterclockwise for the right-handed and clockwise for the left-handed. Move your finger in an upright or vertical oval rather than a circle. Initially, use a larger oval and as you get the timing down, you will use a smaller one.

Before you demonstrate your new skill, ask yourself if you have mushroom for improvement, as you have little margarine for error!

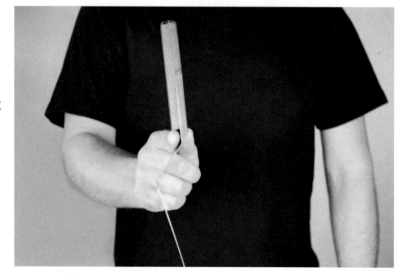

#7 Objectivity

This trick involves placing a book's edge on the back of your hand or wrist, allowing it to tumble toward your fingertips and catching it. The whole trick happens so fast that it looks way more difficult than it is. Most people can be proficient at this trick with just a few practice sessions.

For practice, grab a book about an inch thick. Pick one that stays closed on its own. Practice over a bed or couch. This will limit the damage to the falling book and make it quick for you to grab it again for your next try.

Have your forearm parallel to the floor with your palm facing down. For purposes of explanation, the book has a spine or bound edge, and the opposite side opens to the pages. Place the book across the back of your hand on its opening edge. The book should be perpendicular to your forearm and hand.

Chapter 7

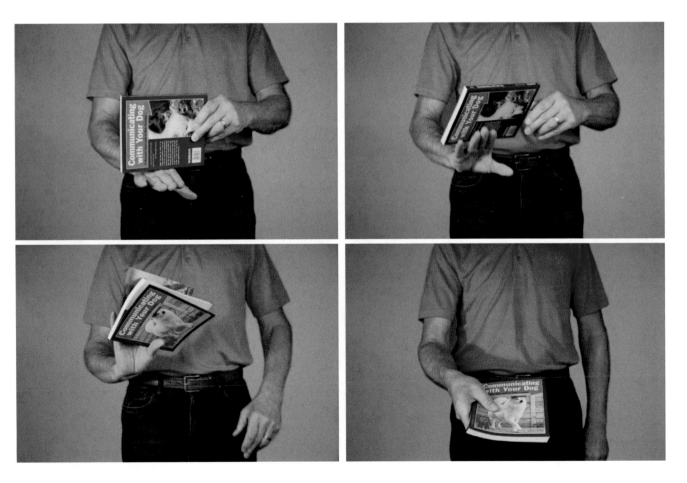

Each book will be positioned on your hand differently depending on its width and thickness. A smaller book will start out closer to the fingertips, while a larger book will move more toward your wrist. The book should be about half the book's width from your fingertips or less. Once you practice a bit, you will be able to grab any book and know where you should start it. It is not critical if the book is off a bit, but error on the side of keeping it closer to your fingertips.

Set the book on your dominant hand. As you release the book, pull your forearm back toward your body. This will cause the book to fall onto your hand and tumble off your fingertips. As the book falls off, reach your hand forward to grab the book between the thumb and fingers of that hand. The book should be wedged between your thumb and four fingers with the palm of your hand still facing down. Now, turn over your wrist as you reach out your hand to present the book.

Get in the habit of having the cover face you at the beginning of the trick. That way the cover will be face up when you present the book at the end.

Once you learn the trick, experiment with books of different size and weight. Hardbound books look better than paperback. For demonstration purposes, avoid heavy or oversized books that would be difficult. The goal is to succeed each time you do the trick in public. Also, avoid immediately repeating the trick. Someone viewing it a couple times might be able to duplicate it.

Although it is a novel idea to use a book, shelve it and start a new chapter using anything else that is flat and can flip off your hand. For example, the check at a restaurant usually comes in a folder. Give it a tumble!

Experiment with different sized plates. Avoid attempts involving antique china or any plate where replacing it would be difficult. Use good judgement and do not do it if you are in a cafeteria, wedding reception or buffet line. Wait until you are holding a plastic plate and are over carpeted floors or grass.

If you play ping-pong, use the trick to hand a paddle to your opponent at the beginning of a match. Place the paddle on its edge with the handle pointing toward your other hand. After you catch the paddle, turn your wrist over, handing the paddle to your opponent. The handle of the paddle should be pointing at your opponent. Let the intimidation begin!

#8 Writing Wrong

In certain situations, you can have some fun while giving your name and phone number to someone requesting it. Maybe use the skill to ask someone out?

To learn how to write your name and phone number upside down, there is less explanation and more practice involved. Grab a piece of paper and a pen or pencil. At the bottom of the paper, neatly write

your name in cursive and your phone number. Turn the paper upside down and use it as your guide. Practice from the first letter in your first name moving right to left, or opposite the normal writing direction. Once you have written your name, turn the paper upside down and check how it looks. Make sure to dot your "i's" and cross your "t's"!

Once you can write your name and phone number upside down, try doing it upside down and backwards, starting with the last letter in your last name.

Advance the skill further, if you like, by being able to write any sentence upside down. You might practice on the sentence that has every letter in the alphabet, "The quick brown fox jumped over the lazy dogs." Or not.

Obviously, demonstrating your new skill is only good in person as it is nothing to write home to Mom about.

#9 Bonding

This trick was demonstrated by the villain in the remake of the Bond movie, <u>Casino Royale</u>. Holding three poker chips in one hand, the front chip is raised and flipped over to be the back chip. This dazzling trick is repeated several times in succession. Unlike other tricks in the book, use this one as much as you like.

To learn the trick, cradle three poker chips in the fingertips of your dominant hand. The index finger and middle finger are supporting the top and side of the three chips while the ring finger is supporting

the bottom of the stack. The little finger is not used. The ring finger exerts pressure against the chips to keep them stable in your fingertips. Once you have the three chips in this position, use the inside edge of your thumb to practice raising and lowering the front chip or the chip closest to the end of your fingers. Having your ring finger on the bottom allows the inside edge of your thumb to connect low on the front chip. The thumb will be able to lift the chip because it is under the side or edge of the chip at this point. The chip should be pressing into the index finger. As you practice raising and lowering the chip, make sure you keep the other two chips stationary.

Once you can move the front chip up and down consistently, the rest of the trick gets easier. Lift the front chip until the center of the chip is at the top of the other two chips. At this point, shift the front chip with your thumb toward the palm of your hand. The chip will flip over and slide down becoming

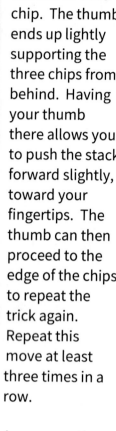

the last or third chip. The thumb ends up lightly supporting the three chips from behind. Having your thumb there allows you to push the stack forward slightly, toward your fingertips. The thumb can then proceed to the edge of the chips to repeat the trick again. Repeat this move at least three times in a row.

As you practice, learn to perform the trick without looking. This makes it more impressive and you will be ready to use it at your next poker game. It is doubtful that your poker buddies will have the Vegas idea how you are doing the trick!

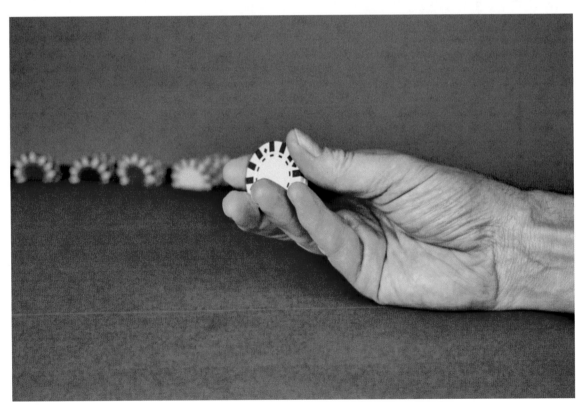

#10 The Invisible Clip

This slick trick is also very practical. The trick allows you to attach several sheets of paper together without using a paperclip or staple. Even if you have a paperclip, it never hurts to show off a little! This is not a flashy trick like others in the book but can really come in handy.

Grab two sheets of paper and tap them to make the edges all line up. While holding the sheets between both hands, fold about an inch of the top left corner of the document down and away from

you at a forty-five-degree angle. This will give you a better-looking final product. Use your fingers to press a good crease on the fold. Next, use your fingertips to make two small tears in the middle of the folded crease, about a quarter inch apart. Fold the torn area down and away from you. It should look like a little square has been cut out. Although, the goal should be to make your work look good, it is not critical as it is still very functional. Depending on your fingertip strength, the length of your

fingernails and the thickness of the paper, most people can attach up to four sheets of paper together at a time.

The simple process is unique. People will be unlikely to see this trick on "pa-per-view". They probably should not see it on a term paper or business presentation, either!

#11 Juggling 101

Everyone should have basic juggling skills. Most people would like to know how to juggle but they just do not have the balls to do it. In this chapter you will learn how to juggle three balls with two hands and two balls with a single hand. Basic juggling looks much harder than it is. In the process of demonstrating both juggling skills, only one ball is up in the air at a time while another ball is just leaving your hand. Things move so fast viewers are always impressed.

For practice, grab three identical items that are round, of the same weight, a good size and have a surface that is easy to grab. Tennis balls are perfect! The web site has a suggested product for beginners.

To learn how to juggle three balls with two hands, stand next to a bed for easy retrieval. Start with one ball in your right hand and one ball in your left. Toss the ball in your right hand up in the air toward your left hand. The toss should form an arc and go about two feet up. As the first ball is coming down, toss the second ball in your left hand to the right and catch the first ball in your left hand. Your left hand tosses the second ball slightly to the inside of the dropping ball. Focus on the ball in the air and use your peripheral vision to catch the dropping ball. As you release the tossed ball, keep your hand open, ready to catch the first ball. Do not worry about the toss you make with your left hand for now, just catch that first ball and stop. Practice this stage of the trick until it seems easy.

For the next stage of the trick, start out with two balls in your right hand. Begin juggling the way you have been practicing, but this time, add one more catch. Focus now on the quality of the toss of the second ball, a two-foot arc to the right. As the second ball is coming down, toss the third ball with your right hand, allowing you to catch the incoming second ball. As soon as you catch the third ball with your left hand recognize that you just need to continue repeating the two stages. One ball will always be in the air and one is getting ready to be tossed.

At this point, make a game out of it, by counting the number of catches you make in a row without dropping a ball.

To juggle two balls with one hand, start by holding two balls in your hand. One is in your palm and the other is out by your fingertips. Toss the ball that is out by your fingertips up into the air, very slightly back toward your body. As it is coming down, allow the other ball to roll onto your fingertips and toss it. Catch the dropping ball with the palm of your hand and repeat the process. Practice until you can keep the juggling going. Just like you did earlier with your practice of juggling three balls, make a game out of how many catches you make in a row without dropping a ball to help you get better quickly.

Once you have the movement down, practice switching between juggling two and three balls. Use other juggling items other than balls, items of different sizes and weights, a mix of objects or while walking. Practice high tosses and low tosses. Allow a high tossed ball to bounce and integrate it into your juggling performance. Low tosses will impress observers with your speed. Although, you are just scratching the surface of juggling, it is always impressive! Warning: avoid juggling knives, chainsaws, lies, girlfriends, etc.

#12 Here's My Card

In the business world, people hand out business cards. In this trick, using sleight-of-hand, a person can present a business card, making it disappear and reappear. If you do not have a business card, create one using your computer, or use other people's cards.

Repetition is the key to learning this skill. The mechanics of the trick are relatively easy, but making the trick look good consistently will take lots of practice. The good news is, once you make some progress on learning the trick you can practice it multiple times per minute without looking. Imagine watching TV while you practice!

Your goals are to perform the trick quickly enough so that the card disappears without being seen. Then, once the card disappears, make sure the card and its corners are hidden.

Hold the card with your palm facing the person to whom you are handing the card, just off your side. Have the front of the card facing the person. Support the card between your straightened index finger

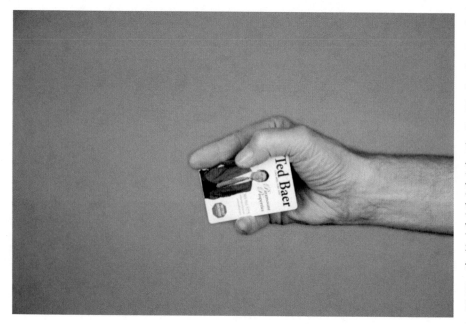

and little finger with your thumb on the face. Have your middle finger and ring finger curled up tightly behind the card and hidden from view. Make the card disappear by quickly thrusting your middle finger and ring finger toward your wrist, and rapidly open your hand while straightening your fingers. Press all four of your fingers together. This will slightly bend the card, helping to hide it behind your hand and pin the card in position. The business card should now be on the backside of your hand being supported by two corners of the card pressed between your index finger and middle finger, and your ring finger and little finger. Initially, the corners will show, but with practice you will learn to barely pin the corners between your fingers.

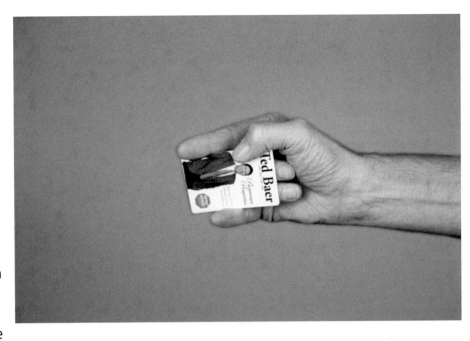

The easy part of the trick is making the card reappear. While making a quick motion with your hand to the side to mask what you are doing, close your hand, bringing the card to the front again. As you grab the card with your thumb, straighten your fingers out to present the card. While learning the first part of the trick, feel free to demonstrate the second part. Just set up the card on the backside of your hand and make it reappear. People will see you pulling your business card out of thin air.

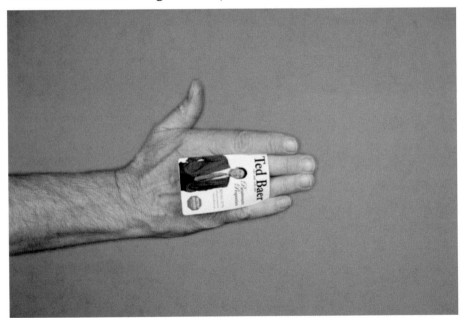

If you have trouble making the card disappear fast enough or hiding the corners of the card, try waving your hand slightly in that section of the trick. Picking a business card that mimics the color of your skin would also help.

It is helpful to practice with various cards once you have the trick down so you can easily perform it using someone else's card. As you are learning the trick, practice in a mirror to help refine it and wait until you have it perfected before using it. Upon reflection, a mirror serves many useful purposes!

#13 Puncture Perfect

This demonstration involves filling a plastic storage or sandwich bag with water and puncturing it using cylindrical items with a point. People will be amazed that the bag does not leak.

Science is your partner in this trick. The flexible plastic of the bag is pushed into each object, creating a temporary seal.

Utilize a sink to practice the trick so you do not make a mess. Grab a storage or sandwich bag with a sealing or locking top. Next grab items like sharpened round pencils, long screws or nails, a piece of a

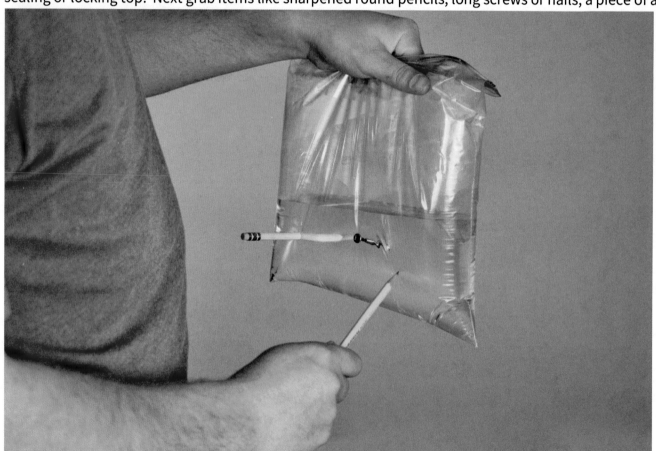

coat hanger with its end cut at an angle, a paperclip, certain pens or other items that have a point to them. Fill the bag three quarters full of water and seal it. Hold the top of the bag with one hand and with the other hand, gently twist the items as you puncture the bag. Try quickly stabbing the first item through the bag for added effect. Take it for, hopefully, a dry run and practice!

Longer items can go all the way through both sides of the bag. That way the bag supports the weight of the item, instead of it dangling from the bag, which could cause a leak. Shorter items, like small nails, can be put through just one side. If you pick small nails, use ones that have a flat head on them. That way you can push them in all the way, literally, nailing the trick!

Any liquid works in the bag. If you want to add additional drama over the Thanksgiving table plan your demonstration wisely for the best results! Use colorful pencils, a couple long nails and one long screw that you screw through the bag to provide a nice variety. People will begin to think of you as punctural, but puncture too many items and your audience may get tired of the hole thing!

#14 Pour Thing

Add a little flair to a common task with this trick. While pouring liquid out of a pitcher, you will elevate the pitcher away from the glass.

Fill a pitcher with water and grab a glass. Place the glass in your kitchen sink to allow for splashing and cleanup, or just go outside. Start low over the glass and pour the water into the center of it. Keep your eyes focused on your target as you raise the pitcher while pouring. The goal is to elevate the pitcher two feet above the glass. Find a happy medium between pouring too slowly and too fast.

Practice your pouring techniques pretending you have a crowded dinner table and you must reach over a row of seated guests or with someone reaching out a glass to you from a seated position. Be creative, instead of demonstrating using a pitcher, use a bottle of wine. Just fill up an empty wine bottle with water to hone your skills.

Be conservative on demonstrating this trick as to how high you go above the glass. A lot will depend on what you are pouring, the shape of the glass and what damage might occur if you miss the glass or splash. If you are pouring water over a resilient table, be more aggressive. Watch when the splatter starts to occur and stop climbing with the pitcher. If you are pouring red wine over your mother-in-law's beautiful dining room table with a white tablecloth, curb the height that you go above the glass. A drop can spell trouble. Always use good judgment, but do not water down the trick!

#15 A Shell Game

This trick involves cracking an egg using one hand instead of two. This is a skill that tons of people have acquired, but one that you should have, as well. Whenever you get near an egg that is begging to be cooked, get ready to practice. It is an easy skill to master. It just depends on how often you eat eggs. If you are one of the cooks in your household, practice every chance you get. If you are not, let the chef know you are scrambling to crack all future eggs until you perfect the skillet or get a bit fried. It is no yolk!

With your palm down, grab an egg in a horizontal position using all five fingers. Position your three middle fingers over the top of the egg, with your little finger and thumb underneath supporting the ends of the egg. To crack the egg, find a narrow, sharp edge as it works better than a wider, rounded one. For instance, a glass is better than a thicker-edged mixing bowl. A good egg cracker can use most anything, even a flat counter. Eventually, you will use the edge of the skillet. For practice, use the edge of a glass. The glass can hold your empty shells.

Now, lightly tap the egg against the edge of the glass until you crack it. Slightly retract the egg, barely rotate it and tap it again. Some cooks will tap the egg several times and others will tap only once. The one tap technique is more dramatic!

Pull your fingers and thumb apart as you open the shell dumping the contents. As you get better, you have two goals. Do not break the yolk and have no shell fragments drop into the skillet. Do make sure to dig out any pieces of shell or the cook will fire you. For the ultimate show off, crack an egg in each hand at the same time!

#16 Smooth Operator

In 1983, a dance move called the backslide was popularized by a pop star and dazzled the world. Renamed the Moonwalk, the dancer creates the illusion of walking forward while sliding backwards. In this chapter, you will learn to Moonwalk which, like many dances, is a "two-step" process.

Initially, the Moonwalk will seem awkward and unnatural for many reasons. The repetitive movement of your legs is unlike any movement you do in life. Plus, your feet are sliding on the floor. Add to this that you are moving backwards and cannot see where you are going! The combined effect is a mesmerizing illusion leaving people wondering how you did it. Most people trying to duplicate the Moonwalk give up quickly. Again, practice, practice, practice to see progress.

Learn this trick wearing socks on a smooth floor or hard-soled shoes on a carpeted floor. It is important that your feet can glide easily across the floor. It is helpful to occasionally practice the Moonwalk next to a floor-to-ceiling mirror for feedback, if possible.

Start with one foot flat on the ground and slightly ahead of the other foot. Elevate the heel of the back foot so that your weight is now on the ball of that foot. Have your knee slightly bent. Slide the flat foot, keeping its heel down, past the bent foot. At this point, three things need to happen

simultaneously. The feet change roles. The sliding foot comes up on its ball, your weight now shifts to this foot and the other foot drops its heel to the floor, ready to begin the slide backwards. Repeat the whole process as now reversed.

To make the Moonwalk look good, the sliding foot needs to keep its heel down throughout the entire glide. The bent foot needs to stay bent while the other foot slides. The more it is bent, the better the moonwalk looks. Extending the distance your sliding foot travels backwards improves the visual. Eventually, try the Moonwalk to music so that you time it properly.

Keep your arms quiet during the Moonwalk, so as not to detract from the movement of your

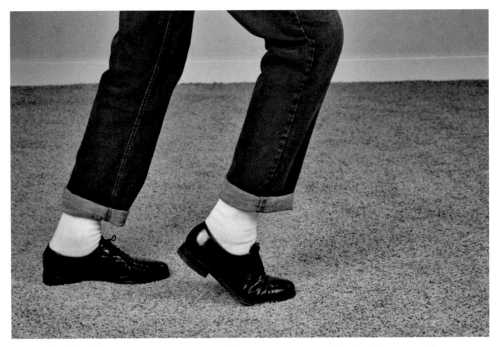

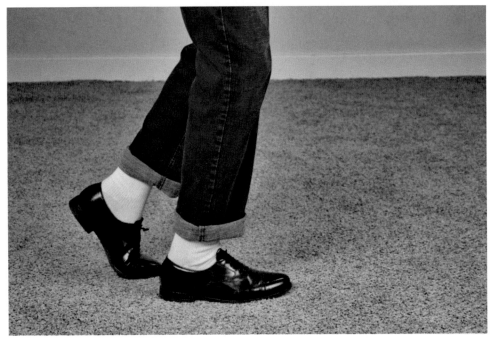

feet. Once you have your balance down, stick your hands in your pocket or keep them by your side.

Generally, your "Moonwalking" space will be limited. Do two slides with each foot and end the move with a spin. To do the spin, cross your rear foot over your front foot. Push off with your toes and allow your flat foot to spin on its ball. Spin 360 degrees and keep dancing!

Do not do the Moonwalk in a crowd until you are completely ready. Use your phone's video camera or have a friend film you to check on your progress. Eventually, you will watch your feat in the video footage!

#17 Pop Fly

The real skill required in this simple trick is recognizing the perfect time to demonstrate it and to subtly pull it off without making a big production of the set up. In this trick, you will launch a ping pong ball by having one in a cup of water and dropping it. The ping pong ball can shoot fifteen feet in the air, or more. Show off the trick whenever you are around a ping pong ball. Since most find table tennis a fun sport and as beer pong is extremely popular, you should have many opportunities.

Take a thick plastic cup or sturdy paper cup. Better yet, cut a recyclable soft plastic water bottle down to about four inches tall. Carry a full water bottle with you and have the modified bottle in your pocket to make the switch. Avoid thin plastic cups or any container that cannot survive a fall. Experiment in advance so that you learn which containers to use. The higher you fill the container with water, the more likely it is to break.

Since you are dealing with water and possibly someone else's house, pick an area appropriate for spilling water. Never use a liquid that could stain or be sticky.

Fill the container with at least an inch of water and up to half filled if you want more power. Drop the ping pong ball in. The ping pong ball will not absorb the water and will float on top. Drop the container carefully with the goal of landing it flat on its bottom for the best results. If the container does not land perfectly flat, the ping pong ball will still shoot, but in a random direction and without much power. If you can, catch the ball nonchalantly without moving since the trick is the launch and not the catch.

The container may be dropped on any surface. You are more likely to break the container on a concrete floor versus a carpeted floor or lawn. If the container breaks, the ping pong ball will not launch and all you get is a big wet spot to clean up! Plus, you have lost your container and the water to quickly repeat the trick. If it does happen, just say "Houston, we have a problem."

#18 Fork Lift

The Fork Trick is a very simple magic trick where you hold a fork in your hand and release it. When you do, viewers are shocked that it does not fall.

Illusionists always find themselves in tricky situations. This trick is only effective if you can hide the palm of your hand, so only demonstrate the trick when your audience is small and across the dinner table from you, or if you are at the end of a dinner table. If your viewers are sitting, you have the added advantage of preventing them from walking behind you, revealing the trick.

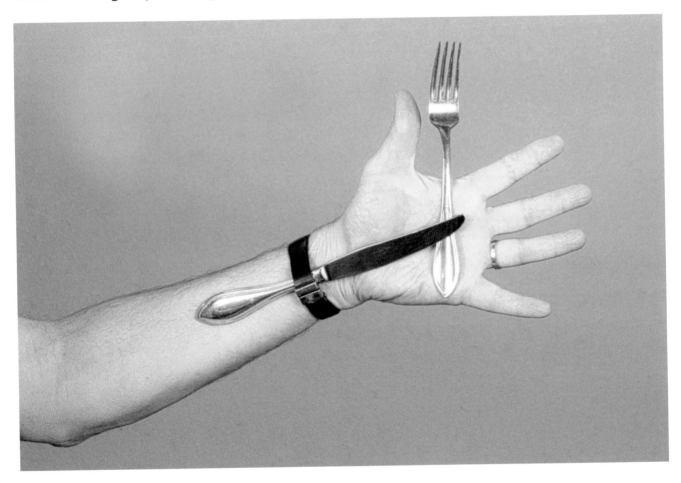

The only advance setup you need for this trick is to wear a watch, bracelet or fitness tracker. Under the dinner table, slip the blade of the knife at your place setting through the band of this item, having the blade extend almost the length of the palm of your hand. The knife's blade needs to be a snug fit against your palm. Do not do the trick with a sharp knife for obvious safety reasons. Use the typical dinner knife and, of course, be careful.

Raise your forearm horizontally in front of you shielding the knife from your audience and with the back of your hand facing out. Have your hand open with your fingers loosely spread. With your free hand, pick up a fork and present it to the crowd, showing that it is a normal fork. Slip the fork behind the tip of the knife as you close your hand as there is no "tine" like the present. Practice to make this action look smooth and normal. The goal is to make your viewers suspicious of your now empty hand, so immediately slide it down your wrist so that it looks like you are using your index finger and middle finger to support the fork. Move it just far enough to where it does not prevent you from opening your fingers on the hand holding the fork. Open your hand up and pause long enough for your audience to jump to the conclusion that your empty hand is supporting the fork, then remove it to the gasps of the crowd. They may not reflect sheer amazement, but at least they will be puzzled!

Practice facing a mirror as presentation is the main skill you are developing here. The trick may be demonstrated sitting down or standing up.

Magicians keep their magic tricks secret for a reason. People tend to be less impressed if they find out how the trick is performed. If you keep this one a secret, you may get a request from a fan down the road to repeat it. Never repeat the trick immediately as you need the crowd gasp to end the trick.

#19 Wild Card

Common among people who practice card tricks, a single playing card is spun on the middle finger. In this chapter, you will learn using a playing card then transfer the skill to a credit card. The credit card will give you more opportunity to use your new skill and is smaller than a playing card, solving any clearance issues if you have smaller hands.

Grab a playing card and cut it down to the size of a credit card. Position your hand with your palm tilted at a forty-five-degree angle. Lightly pinch the card between your thumb and your middle finger, with your middle finger centered under the card. The card will rest on the inside tip of your middle finger.

Initially, practice balancing the card just on your middle finger while moving your hand around a bit. Try to keep the card level throughout the trick. Adding a little moisture to your middle finger will keep the card from sliding off while making it slippery.

The card will be propelled by your index finger. For the initial training, it helps to put a light coating of rubber cement on the tip of your index finger for traction. Be careful not to get the cement on your other fingers. You will not need the cement once you start learning the trick.

The index finger is positioned under the card next to your middle finger. Initially, just practice moving the card back and forth using your index finger. Turn the card counterclockwise approximately an inch and quickly pull the card back clockwise. Both actions are using your index finger to move the card. If you are left-handed, start moving the card clockwise and pull the card back counterclockwise. Think of this move as winding up, giving your index finger more power as the finger has a little more distance to travel. While most of the movement is done with the index finger, you will find that the middle finger moves slightly away from you, the thumb pulls in a bit and there is a very small flick of the wrist.

Place the slightest pressure between your thumb and middle finger. Think about a light touch and balancing the card.

Once you get good at this movement, wind up, flick your index finger back quickly as you simultaneously release your thumb, allowing the playing card to spin balanced on your middle finger.

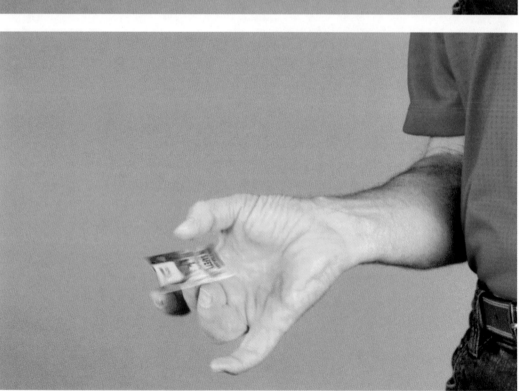

Most will find that after twenty tries or more, you will achieve a small victory with the card spinning a half turn or more. This will show you that the trick is possible and give you confidence to keep practicing until you perfect your new skill. Mark the top of the card so you can get an idea of how far it rotates. Concentrate holding the card lightly and on the timing of the release.

Once you get the trick down, transfer your abilities to a credit card. The credit card has a slippery bottom perfect for spinning. Since it is heavier than a playing card, work on the initial move to propel the card and take it for a spin. Enjoy the irony of getting credit every time you use your credit card but realize that you have had a big hand in your success!

#20 Welcome To the Club

Made famous by Tiger Woods in a Nike Golf commercial, Tiger bounces a golf ball on the face of his club demonstrating his total control over the ball. With some repetition, you can do it, too.

Grab your pitching wedge or another club that has its face very laid back. Pick a safe place to practice preventing damaging things. A grassy area with tall grass has advantages as you can slip your clubface under the ball and pop it up into your hand. It also keeps you from having to bend over with each miss. On carpeting, you can use the inside of your foot and the edge of the club to trap the ball and launch it into the air. Just raise your foot and lift the club. Launch it about a foot into the air and use your clubface to bounce the ball up higher so you can grab it. As with all the tricks in this book, use caution. It is a fore-gone conclusion that a golf ball can hurt!

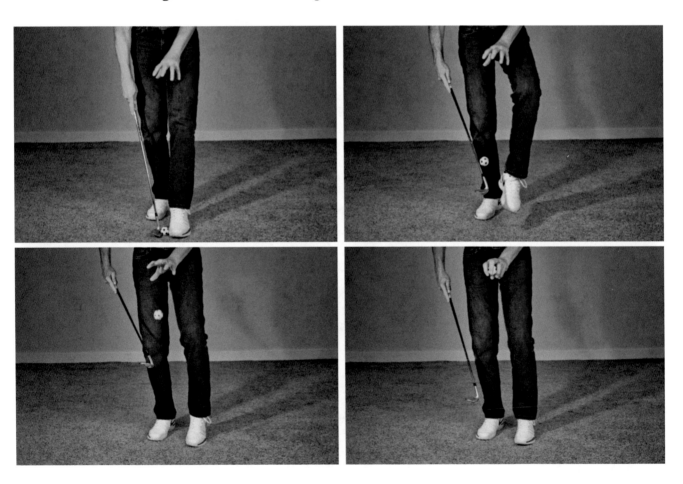

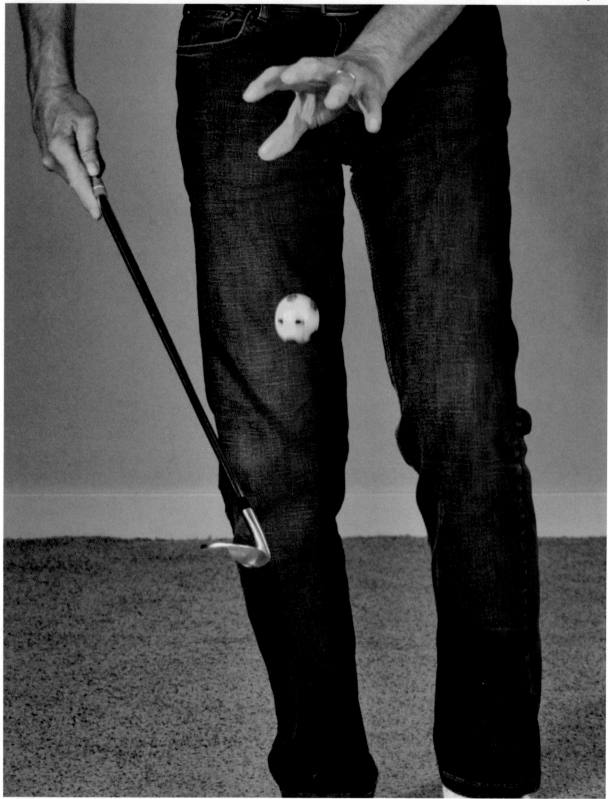

Stand holding the club comfortably in one hand toward the lower portion of its grip. The shaft can run up under your forearm for support or be sticking out a bit. Try to keep your grip relaxed. Flatten the clubface up by rotating the club in your grip. The goal is to make the face parallel to the ground so that you can bounce the ball straight up in the air. As you practice, you will see that it is crucial to keep the clubface level or flat to get the control you need. Also, try to keep the clubface close - about a foot away from your body. Keeping the ball bouncing close to your body will add to your control, offering a more consistent arm movement and line of sight to the clubface. Since you never take your eyes off the ball, you need to use your peripheral vision to keep track of the club face. The goal throughout the trick is to have the ball strike the center of that clubface.

Start by dropping the ball on to the face of the club. The ball's momentum will cause it to bounce off the face. As the momentum fades, move the clubface upwards just before the ball makes contact again. Keep your wrist locked while slightly moving your arm up and down. Work at bouncing the ball about eight inches off your clubface. If you bounce it higher than that, you make the trick more difficult to learn. Also, if you start losing control of the bouncing ball, stop and start again. Just bounce the ball up higher, grab it and start over.

To encourage your progress, count the number of times you can bounce the ball. Start each practice session with a clean slate and set a realistic goal to bounce the ball a certain number of times. Once you accomplish your goal, quit on a positive note. Demonstrate your trick by bouncing the ball about ten times, then bounce it higher in the air and grab it.

If you want to take the trick further, head to the web and watch Tiger's and other professional golfers' trick skills. In general, practice the fancier elements of the trick separately before you start combining them. In your practice sessions, make a little progress on each element and stop on a high note. That will leave you excited for your next practice session.

Learn how to pop the ball up higher to give you time to transition between elements, but realize the higher you go, the harder it will be to keep the ball bouncing.

Try using your non-dominant hand and arm for several bounces before transitioning to your dominant arm. Unless you tend to be ambidextrous, this will be a lot harder to learn, but you can impress people by using a few bounces. To accomplish this, practice the basics until you can do three or four bounces consistently with your non-dominant hand, then move the club quickly to your dominant hand while keeping the ball bouncing. As you succeed in switching hands, you will feel a rush of relief as you control the club with your more capable side!

Another thing you can practice is "catching" the golf ball on your clubface. As you are bouncing the ball, stop your arm action and allow the clubface to absorb any momentum and inertia the ball has. Balance the ball on your clubface for a second then launch it up in the air to continue your routine.

When you demonstrate your skills, stick to the elements of the trick that you have conquered. That would be par for the course!

#21 Do You Mind?

Among the easiest tricks in the book is using your mind to roll a straw across a table. This skill can be learned in a few minutes. The word, "mentally", is used loosely. The goal is to make it look like the straw is being moved with your awesome telekinetic powers.

To practice this trick, sit down at a table or other smooth surface with a straw placed parallel to you. Put your hand about four inches on the other side of the straw. Have the tips of your fingers and thumb open and pointed back toward the straw. Simultaneously and subtly, blow the straw slowly across the table while keeping your hand the same distance in front of the straw. Give the effect that you are pulling the straw by slowly closing your fingertips. This works as a distraction, as well.

Remember, you are practicing a performance. Blow the straw lightly so that you can keep your hand out in front of it properly until it stops. Blowing the straw past your fingers wrecks the trick. Open your lips just slightly and try not to make it look like you are blowing. Keep your head motionless and in a normal position. It helps if the room is somewhat noisy to mask the sound of you blowing.

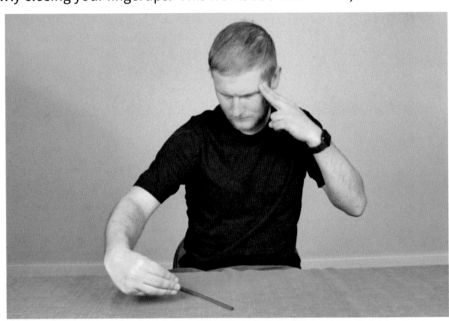

When demonstrating this mind over matter, draw some interest by clearing a path for the straw. Get people's attention and set the stage. Grab the straw with the same hand that you will be using to pull the straw. Hold it vertically in front of your face for just a second. Intently look at the straw as you place it on the table and continue to stare at it. Pretend that your initial attempt to pull the straw fails and shake your head. Try it a second time with success. As with many of the skills you have learned in this book, repeating the feat will diminish its effect.

Kids love this trick! All should find it breathtaking. If you are having trouble utilizing your telekinetic powers, perhaps you are a bit thought less.

#22 No Solstice Required

This is an easy trick that will eggcite many due to the common misconception that you can only balance an egg on its end certain days of the year. Those days would be the spring and fall equinox, where there is no tilt of the earth as compared to the sun, and on the winter and summer solstice where there is the maximum tilt of the earth as compared to the sun. In realty, an egg may be balanced on its end 365 days of a year.

Grab several raw eggs from your refrigerator. Try to find ones with a defined bottom and top. These are usually easier to balance than others. Balancing an egg requires a steady hand and patience, so sitting down while you are practicing is suggested. Once you get the hang of it, you will be able to do it standing up. Any sturdy counter or tabletop will do. Although there may be some advantage to picking a rougher surface like a wooden tabletop over a smooth granite countertop, either will work.

Grab an egg with both hands. Rest the edges of your palms on the table. Support the egg vertically using your fingers in the back and your thumbs on the front of the egg. The wider end of the egg should be touching the table, lowering its center of gravity. If you were looking straight down on the egg as if it was a clock, put your fingers at the 1:30 and 10:30 positions, and your thumbs in the 4:30 and 7:30 positions. Hold the egg loosely at these four points. Let your fingers act as a frame to keep the egg upright until it balances. The egg will seem to do everything it can to resist balancing, until it does. It will seem just as magical every time you balance an egg as it does the first time. Once you get the hang of it, practice on different surfaces and with different eggs to allow you to do the trick quickly.

Take the trick to the next level by grabbing a cutting board and propping up the end of it. Have a slope of approximately an inch drop per foot of the cutting board. Recognize that you will ignore the slope and balance the egg so that it is pointing to the ceiling, as usual. It is easy to accomplish, and you will look like an egg-spert!

#23 Up In Arms

This is a variation on a trick that you may have seen performed. The standard demonstration involves dropping a ball on to your bicep muscle, and having the muscle launch the ball upwards to be caught by the same hand. This variation is that you will bounce the ball twice off your bicep before catching it. This makes the trick a bit fresher.

Practicing over a non-carpeted floor is helpful, but not necessary. It makes it easier to retrieve a missed ball on the bounce.

Grab several sized balls that are approximately two to seven inches in diameter. Practicing with different balls prepares you for any size ball you might come across. Hold the ball and raise your elbow until it is pointed forward or a bit out to the side. The upper arm is not quite parallel to the ground. Set your forearm at more than a right angle to your upper arm, with the forearm tilting slightly back toward your body. Since you are dropping the ball on to your bicep, twist your wrist so that the ball is directly over your bicep.

Drop the ball onto your bicep as you straighten your arm quickly. When you straighten, the upper arm moves up rapidly, striking the ball. Practice doing one bounce on the bicep until you are proficient, then go for two bounces. Each time, your outstretched hand should catch the ball.

Start by popping the ball straight up in the air about six inches so that you can launch it a second time back into your hand. In between bounces, reload your arm by returning it to the initial position so that you can straighten it again. Watch the ball carefully for greater success. The first pop should not be as aggressive as the second one. Although most viewing this trick will think that you are launching it with your muscle, no muscle is required and having a well-defined muscle may make the trick harder. Experiment to find the best place on your arm to initially drop the ball. It may be the inside of your elbow.

Think creatively with all the movements you learn in this book. If a ball is not readily available, crumple a piece of paper into a ball or use an orange to demonstrate your skills. People think oranges are very a-peeling!

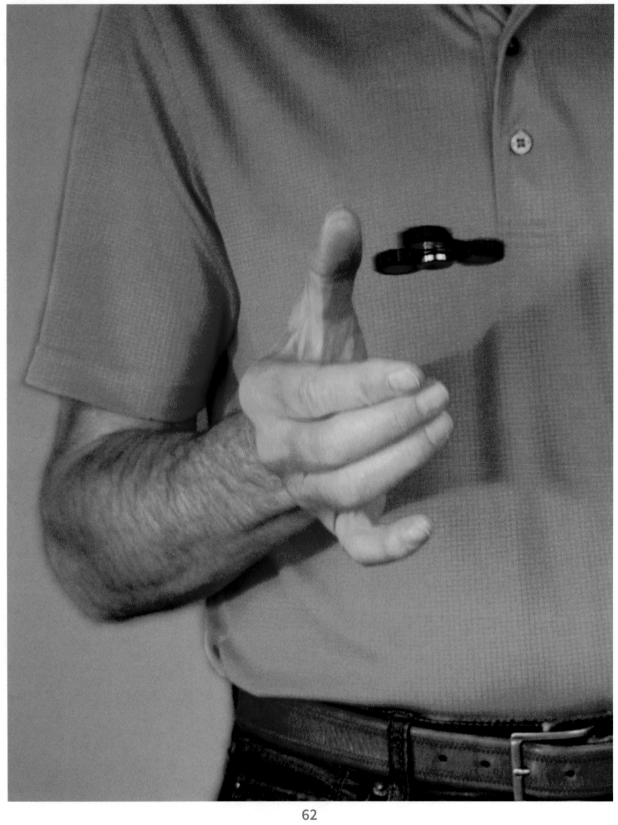

#24 Take It For a Spin

When the Fidget Spinner hit the market, having over 200 million in sales in 2017, it was heralded as the hottest toy in the industry. The device was designed for users who fidget and marketed as

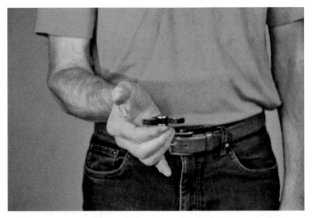

an aid to expend excess nervous energy. It is supposed to reduce stress. The captivating spinning device works like a gyroscope with bearings in a center circular pad or axis. Most people just spin them and balance them on a finger, but there are many tricks that can be done with them. Three are covered here.

No question, your Fidget Spinner will be dropped many times, so sit down or do the trick over a bed or couch until you get proficient.

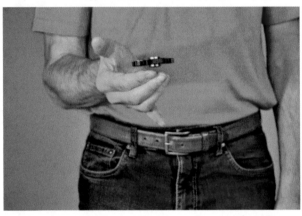

In the Three Finger Transfer, the spinning Fidget Spinner moves from the index finger to the middle finger and then to the ring finger. Start by holding the spinner on the center pad between your index finger and thumb with the palm of your hand facing up but tilted slightly toward you. Spin the device and release your thumb, balancing the device on your fingertip. Initially, practice gently bouncing the spinning device up and down on your index finger. Toss the spinner in the air so that it just barely leaves your index finger. Once you are good at this, it is time to move the spinner between fingers. Get the device spinning on your index finger and "bounce" it up while moving your middle finger under it. Concentrate on catching the center of the spinner on your middle finger pad. Bounce your hand up again, moving the Fidget Spinner to the ring finger pad.

The Upward Toss involves throwing the Fidget Spinner up in the air spinning parallel to the ground and catching it as it continues to spin. Start in the same position that you started above in the Three Finger Transfer. Spin the device and move your forearm up and down. Barely release your grip on the device simultaneously with both your index finger and

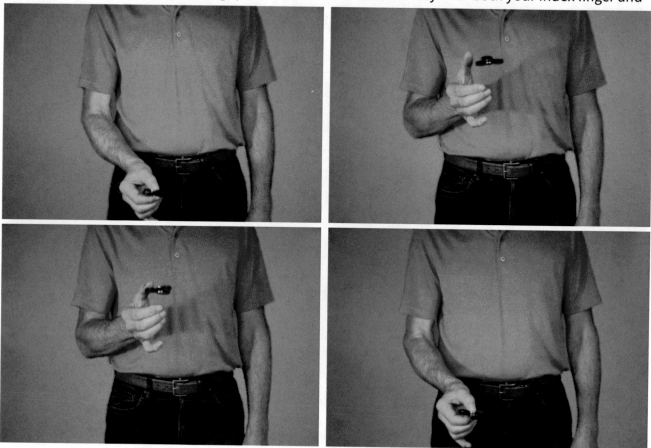

thumb tossing it in the air. With practice lengthen the distance that you are throwing the Fidget Spinner. Concentrate on the design or insignia on the center pad, as it stays stationary. If you do not have something to concentrate on, add a sticker and draw an "X" on it. Do not look at the spinning arms. Keep all your other fingers out of the way. Often your index finger is not curved enough and may get in the way, as well.

The Sideways Toss simply involves tossing the spinning Fidget Spinner between your hands. Start in the same position as the other tricks, but this time toss the device a noticeably short distance toward your other hand. Keep the spinner flat or parallel to the ground as you toss it. Catch it between your thumb and index finger. With practice, increase the distance of the toss.

It helps to have a Fidget Spinner that has center pads that are concave. The web site has a suggested one to buy.

Chapter 24

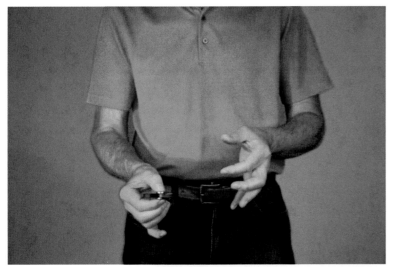

With all three tricks, it is more important keeping the Fidget Spinner spinning than how fast you make it spin. Realize where you make your mistakes so that you can correct them to advance your skills quickly. Lastly, work on combining the tricks back to back. Whenever you feel fidgety, you will be able to take this trick out for a spin and give a little demo of your amazing skills. Assume your rightful place as air apparent!

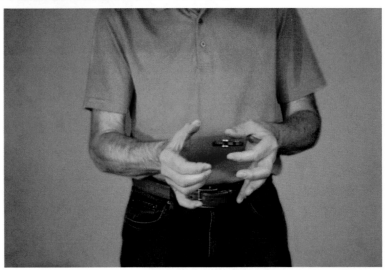

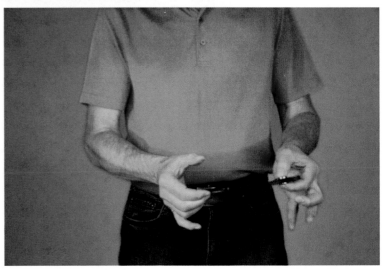

#25 Trying Tying

Being able to tie a few good knots puts you ahead of the crowd. There are hundreds of useful knots. A showy one that will impress your friends is called a Monkey's Fist. It is named so because the knot resembles a fist with fingers. The Monkey's Fist is generally tied at the end of a rope and serves as a weight, making it easy to throw. The nautical community uses it in several capacities, but mainly to throw a line to shore or to another boat. It is quite the accomplishment to learn how to tie the knot as it is hard to learn from written instructions or pictures. Try not to be frustrated with the instructions. Your attempts at learning the knot will only help you understanding it. Assume that it will be learning by trial and error.

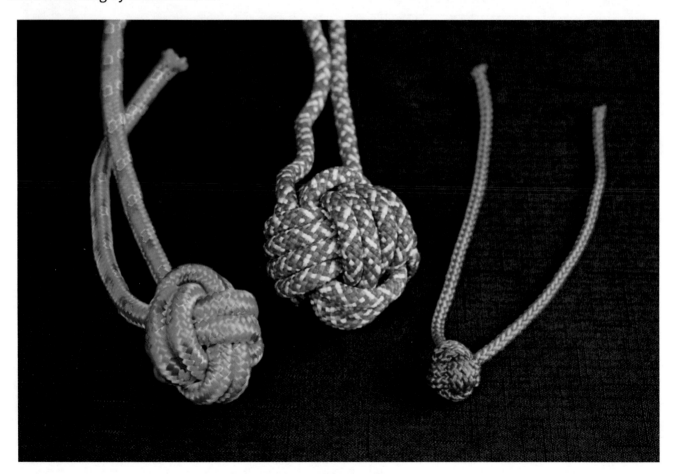

Grab a piece of cord or rope. The more pliable the better. The colorful polypropylene ropes are tough on beginners. The length will depend on how many loops you use and the width of the rope. For training, practice doing two loops of rope on each of the six sides. Later you can work on three, four and even five loops. Although three loops seem to be the minimum Monkey Fist you see in decorative items like key chains, even two loops will impress people.

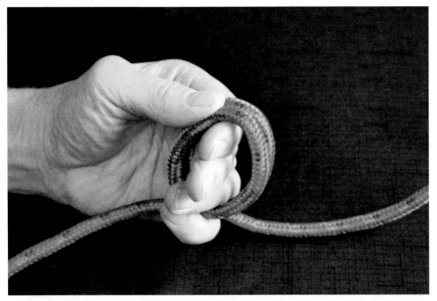

For a two loop Monkey Fist, use a four-foot length of rope and grab it about one foot from an end. The goal is to make two sets of loops going three different directions, up and down, front to back and side to side. For the first step, have your left hand open with your palm facing you and your thumb up. Pin the rope between your thumb and the inside of your hand. The shorter part of the rope is dangling next to your palm. The longer part of the rope is dangling over the top edge of your left index finger and is going down the backside of your fingers. The longer part of the rope is the working end that you will be using until the knot is formed, but not tightened. Make one loop around your first three fingers bringing the rope toward you as if you were going to wrap it around again. Now, have the little finger support the short rope pointing away from you and the long end pointing toward you. At this point, you should have two ropes running next to each other on the outside and inside of your left hand. Grab

the top of the ropes with your right hand to allow you to pinch the bottom of the loops with the index finger and thumb of your left hand. Slip all but your index finger out of the loops and adjust them to be equal in size, if necessary.

Using the working end of the rope, make another two loops around and perpendicular to the two loops you just made. It is important that you circle the outside of the existing two loops in the correct direction. Take the working end of the rope directly toward the back of your left-hand circling

clockwise. Circle the rope twice, ending with the rope pointing away from you. Make sure to circle around the short end of the rope. If you do miss it, you can later thread it through the knot you made before tightening.

For the third step, pin your work down on a table or knee, on its side. Take the working end of the rope and thread it through the upper loops leaving no slack. These are the two initial loops you made

that are now facing away from you. Then pull the rope back completely through the lower loops or those loops closest to you. As you do this, make sure to release the one rope that you initially supported with your little finger that pointed toward you. This will allow two ropes to be on that side of the eventual knot. Repeat the threading process a second time, going through the upper loop and through the lower loop. Finally, go back through the upper loop for a third time.

It is critical that, throughout the entire process of looping the rope, that the loops be next to each other. Do not let the ropes cross over each other as you wind and thread the loops.

It is a complicated knot that will require some patience learning. Once you complete the loops, you are left with a seemingly unorganized mess that needs to be tightened. Do not lose heart - you will be rewarded seeing your beautiful work come together into a great looking knot.

The goal in tightening the rope is to do it slowly over multiple stages. Start with those loops that are not connected to the loose ends of the rope, working from the middle set of loops out. Pull on one of the ropes in that middle set of loops creating a bit of slack and rotate the knot continuing to pull the same rope until the slack is gone. Repeat the process with all the loops until you are done. During the tightening process, keep the ropes from crossing. Depending on the number of loops you do and the thickness of the rope, a little screwdriver may help you tighten the knot near completion.

After you get proficient at tightening the knot, you have two other options you can try. Stick a rock, marble, small ball or other round item inside the knot before tightening. This helps hold the shape of the knot and reduces the amount of tightening needed. The object needs to be small enough so that once the knot is tightened, the object is not visible. The original knot was not intended to have an item placed inside it, but it works well.

Another option that you have before tightening is to take the last thread you made with the rope and unthread it. Tie a knot in this section of rope near your monkey fist. Cut the end of the rope off, tuck the little knot inside the center of the monkey fist and then tighten all the loops around it. The final product will be a rope with a monkey fist on the end.

Since tying the Monkey Fist is a several-minute event, demonstrate it when you have a little time on your hands. Just keep a length of cord or rope in your backpack or jacket pocket for when you take a break on a hike, are sitting around a campfire or taking a break at work.

If you have enjoyed learning this knot, try learning the very practical Bowline. This very sturdy knot can be subjected to a huge load, yet easily untied. As with learning any new knot, it helps to be taut!

#26   A Show of Hands

A simple magic trick that will amaze is making a toothpick disappear. With minimal practice, even a termite will be impressed.

Tools include a couple toothpicks and some scotch tape. Put a small piece of tape on the end of the toothpick and stick it to the middle of your thumb nail. Have the toothpick run in line with your thumb, pointing toward your hand. Twist out the toothpick leaving a little pocket that will later hold the toothpick.

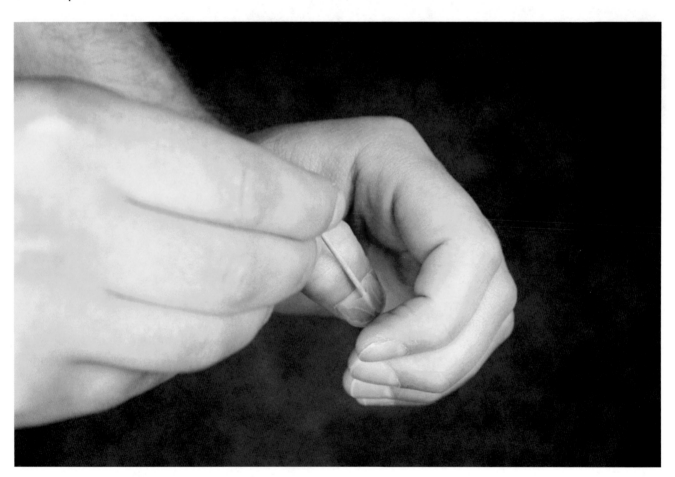

When you demonstrate this trick, start by showing that it is a normal toothpick. Slowly start to close your other hand into an upright fist with the back of your thumb facing the sky. As you are closing your hand, tuck your thumb nail into the fist as you slip the toothpick into the little pocket you made with the tape. Use your closing fingers to hide the tape on the back of your thumb from your viewers. Apply just a little pressure to the tape and toothpick by squeezing your fist.

Practice your showmanship by creating a distraction by blowing on your hand, or either waving or snapping your fingers on the other hand as you open your fist quickly. Both hands should be open at this point with your palms facing your audience at about a forty-five-degree angle showing that the toothpick has disappeared. Wiggle your fingers, if you like, but do not wiggle your thumb as the toothpick might show. Practice in front of a mirror until you get the trick down.

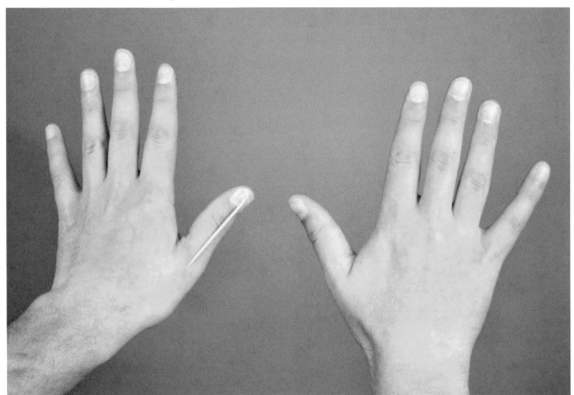

Optionally, you can make the toothpick reappear, or hide the toothpick and grab another toothpick from the table to demonstrate the trick a second time. Magicians never reveal their secrets. It would take away all the fun! When they ask how you did it, tell them that the trick was a piece of cake and lettuce resume dinner!

Although this trick may be demonstrated anywhere, restaurants are ideal as they have toothpicks at the front door. Just grab two or three on the way in. The trick is only effective when you can hide the toothpick, so only demonstrate it when your audience is small and across the table from you. You can carry a small piece of tape on the back of your cell phone and set up the trick quietly in your lap. Attach the tape to your cell phone, bending a corner for easy removal. That way you can grab the tape discreetly.

#27 Liquidation

History books are filled with famous women and men who did remarkable things. Of their vast and varied skills, none of them were ever documented squirting water. This is your chance to create history. Typically executed in a pool or hot tub, but at your disposal with any body of water like a sink, fountain or creek, you will squirt someone with water collected in your clenched hands.

Since most of us do not have a pool to practice in, you need a bathtub, bucket, large kitchen bowl, pot or other container to hold water. The container must be deep and wide enough to submerge both your locked hands up to your wrists. Fill your bucket with warm water for your own comfort. Be prepared to get wet so practice in an area that can handle a soaking. Outside is the perfect choice or you can practice in the bathtub or shower.

Initially, practice without the water. Although you will not get the feedback you eventually need, you can practice putting your hands in the correct position. Put both your palms together and interlock or lace your fingers. Wrap your thumbs around, as well. Make sure the pads on your palms are offset a bit. The goal is to create the largest water reservoir you can inside of your hands while preventing water from leaking out. Examine your hands for obvious leaks and adjust, as necessary. Push your palms together hard and listen for the air escaping. The air should escape near the little fingers on the outside edge of the hand. The squirt will come from there. Once you feel you have the hand position down, start practicing with water.

Submerge your entwined hands, allowing the water to seep inside from the top, displacing the air. Clench your hands and raise them out of the water to practice keeping the water inside them. If water is leaking out, adjust your hands. The proper technique does involve some finger strength. Once your hands can hold the water, it is time to shoot the water!

Raise your hands toward your chin, twisting your wrists back toward you so that you are aiming the right direction. When the outside edge of your hands is pointing away from you, push your palms together hard. It happens quickly but try to initiate the push from the thumb side of your locked hands. Work on getting a little water to squirt out of the proper spot on your hands by your little fingers. Once you get some water squirting from the correct spot, you can work on getting the squirt to go six feet or more. Reload after every squirt.

Once you have acquired this skill, wait until you run across the right water source and proper situation. Then, be like a vampire and find your necks victim!

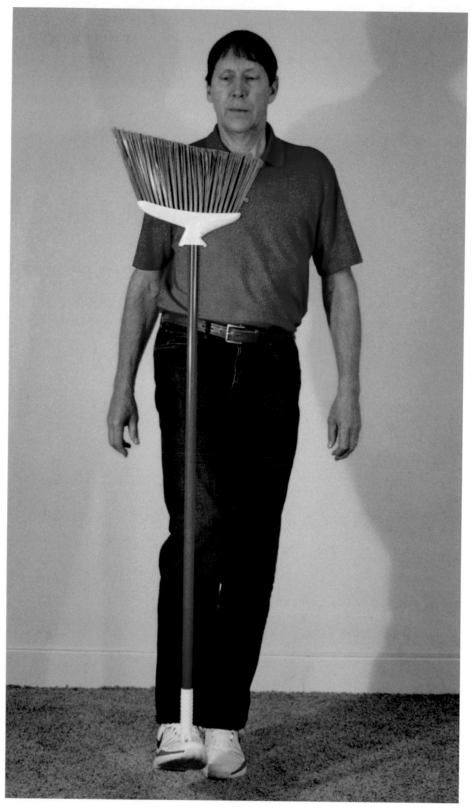

#28 Live Footage

It is said that, "life is a balancing act", so learning this trick will guarantee you a 51% chance of improving your future. In this trick, you will balance an object on the top of your foot, while balanced on the other leg.

The first job is to pick an object to balance. Initially, selecting something long that is heavier on one end will make it easier to learn. Scientifically, it has to do with larger rotational inertia caused by moving the center of the mass farther away from your foot. In layman's terms, the farther the weight is away from your foot, the slower it will fall over. The slower it falls over, the more time you have to adjust your foot to rebalance the object. It helps to practice with something long enough to allow you to grab it before it falls – like a kitchen broom. Once you get the trick down, you can use an umbrella, a baseball bat, a stick in the forest or any other items that fit the bill.

By the way, you will benefit even more when you demonstrate your new skill because the typical observer will think that it is tougher to balance an object that has its heavier end up, instead of down. Typically, you want a lower center of gravity.

Start balancing the broom with your hand. It will be considerably easier than using your foot, but a good introduction. Once you get the feel for that, place the broom handle on the top of your foot just behind where your toes bend. If you do not have shoes on, pull your toes back to make a "pocket" to hold the end of the broom. Initially, hold on to a wall or table so you can concentrate on keeping the broom balanced. If the top of the broom is heading your direction, pull your foot in the same direction. Keep adjusting your foot to remain under the top of the broom. Work to keep the top of the broom quiet and steady so that your adjustments are minor. As you get the hang of it, stop holding on to something for balance. When the balancing foot gets tired and you experience the agony of 'da feet, switch feet. Eventually, you will have a favorite side to use for demonstration.

#29 Whip It, Whip It Good

Popularized by Josh Womack, a second-round draft pick of the Mariners, a baseball bat is swung, released and spun three hundred and sixty degrees during the swing. The batter releases the bat mid swing and catches the handle before ending the swing. It is an impressive trick since the spinning bat is moving quickly enough to where the eye has trouble following it.

Pick an outside location to practice, away from anything that can be damaged. Before practicing or attempting to perform this trick, review the instructions carefully, and make sure the area around you is clear of any persons, pets or objects that might be injured or damaged if you lose control of the bat. A dangerous trick to learn, please use extreme caution. Grab your football helmet, mouth guard, cup, shin protectors, gloves and any other protective gear that you have. An air-filled Sumo suit might not be a bad idea! For safety, start off with a plastic wiffleball bat until you get good at the trick, then go to a wooden or metal baseball bat with bubble wrap padding the wider, last eighteen inches of

the bat. Just tape it on. Take your time graduating to an unwrapped bat. Bruise a bone, and you will feel it to marrow!

Practice making a normal forward swing with the bat, but as your hands reach your front hip quickly

reverse the direction of your hands backward and let go of the bat. The handle of the bat rapidly spins back from where it just came. Done correctly, the fingers of both hands are pointing toward the rear of your stance.

Understanding the science behind this trick will help you learn it. The end of the bat is wider, heavier and travels a farther distance with more speed than the handle of the bat. Use the built-up momentum of the end of the bat to spin it around, catch the handle and finish the swing. Be careful not to spin the bat back toward you. The main momentum of the bat is moving forward toward the infield, so the revolving bat should keep moving in that direction if you miss grabbing it. With your initial attempts, worry more that the spinning bat is heading any direction other than back toward you and less about catching it. This is where you can get hurt.

As the bat is spinning around, be prepared to catch the handle of the bat and finish the swing. You will get the swing of it quickly and the trick will be a real hit right off the bat!

#30 Stick Together

Over twenty-five percent of the world's population uses chopsticks daily. Many other people in the world select chopsticks to eat certain foods. Categorized more as a skill than a trick, chopsticks are fun and easy to use. As a reader of this book, you should use chopsticks when a restaurant offers them.

To learn how to use chopsticks you need a pair. Most large grocery store chains sell them or, when you go out for Chinese food, bring home a disposable pair. The quality of the chopsticks does not matter. Fancier ones are smoother, look better, last longer and are easier to clean. The web site has suggested ten pair of high-quality fiberglass chopsticks for under $10. Let your family in on the fun!

There are several different techniques for using chopsticks. Practice initially without food. Tear six or seven strips of paper. Crumple each paper strip making wads of variable sizes. Make some small ones to challenge your skills. Mix in some uncooked noodles or other items, if you like.

The chopsticks are cradled much like you hold a pen. The first, or lower, chopstick is placed in the "V" created by your thumb and index finger. The ring finger fingertip applies pressure to the chopstick about two to three inches up from the bottom end. It is wedged between the fingertip of the ring finger and the lower portion of your thumb. If you have a fingernail on the ring finger, use the edge of it to steady the stick. This chopstick remains in the same position throughout its use and is stationary.

The second, or upper chopstick, is held between fingertips of the index finger, middle finger and the thumb. This is the chopstick that moves. Move it with your index finger and middle finger while your thumb stays still. The index finger and middle finger move in tandem, exerting slight pressure against the thumb.

When you hold both chopsticks, the end of the upper chopstick sticks out a bit past the lower chopstick. This will help you grab things that are out in front of you. If you loosen your grip slightly on the chopsticks, you can adjust how far the chopsticks stick out by putting their tips down onto a hard surface like a plate or table.

Practice grabbing and moving around the paper wads you made. Once you have the basics down, practice eating with chopsticks for a few meals. The progress will be quick as you get a reward with every correct grab of food. You may be a little slow in the beginning, but you will make like mustard, catch up and relish in your new skill. In the end, you will be left wonton for more.

#31 Third Time's a Charm

This feels more like an amazing feat than a trick! Once you balance three golf balls, you cannot help but be impressed with yourself!

Balancing three golf balls requires a steady hand and patience, so sit down while you do this trick. Any counter or tabletop will do, if it is close to level and steady. Although there may be some advantage to picking a rougher surface like a wooden table or granite counter, over a Formica counter, either will work. This time it will be useful to be counter productive!

Grab three golf balls. They can be of mixed brands, although there is an advantage to using brands that have larger dimples on them. When you are demonstrating the trick, be confident. It is a tough trick, but practice will give you that confidence.

Most golf balls have various sized dimples on them. Place your first golf ball down on the table and allow it to seek its own resting point. Hopefully, it will stop on a larger dimple, providing a sturdy

base. Balancing the second ball is easy. Grab the second golf ball with both hands and rest the edges of your palms on the table. Support the golf ball from the backside using your index and middle finger from both hands, and your thumbs on the front of the ball. Looking straight down on the golf ball, as if it were a clock, have your fingers in the 1:30 and 10:30 positions, and your thumbs in the 4:30 and 7:30 positions. Lower the second ball onto the first ball. Rotate it slightly until it balances and then release your grip. Look to see if you have a large dimple on the top. If you do not, rotate the ball to balance so there is a big dimple at the top. This will be the base for the third ball.

Once you have two balls balanced, it can save you time to test its sturdiness. Place your index finger on the very top of the second ball. Carefully press down on the balls. This will give you an idea if they are stable enough to support a third ball. If you press down and the two balls fall, start over. A firm base is needed to proceed.

Balancing the third ball is the challenge. Ever so carefully, lower the supported third ball onto the balanced second ball. Make sure the third ball is balanced before you release it. If it is not, delicately use the contact of the third ball to steady the two below before repositioning the third ball. This will save you from having to start over once you get the touch. The trick has its ups and downs, but with practice, you will develop the skill of saving the two balanced balls. Just as with the second ball, rotate the third ball slightly until it balances.

Once you can balance three golf balls, work on different surfaces and with different golf balls. Practice so that you can do the trick in under a minute. Try your best to be humble.

#32 There Must Be a Catch

When you see someone catch something behind their back, it is impressive. This is an easy skill to learn and you will have quick success with a little practice.

Choose a durable object that will fit into the palm of your hand and that can sustain being dropped. Pick an object that will not damage the floor or furniture when dropped. Even after you get the trick down, always be conscious of the damage you might accidentally cause.

Initially, grab something about the size of a tennis ball. Hold it in your dominant hand about a foot away from your bellybutton. Toss it up and over your head. The ideal toss should slightly clear your head and come down within inches of your back. Lean forward if your toss has the height but may not

clear the back of your head. A good toss sets up an easy catch. Use your other hand to make the catch. Place your hand palm up next to the small of your back with your fingers out as wide as possible. Have your forearm slightly away from your back, but not far enough away to allow the object to fall through the gap. Since the trick happens behind your back, your audience will never see how pretty the catch is so you can get away with a sloppy snag. If you trap the object between your forearm and your back, pull your hand to the side, scooping it up.

Watch the tossed object and try to position your hand where you guess the object will land. Anticipate the time it will take for the object to fall and be ready to close your hand around it.

Once you get the trick down, try various sized items. Catching the object with the same hand that throws it looks more difficult and many find it easier to do. You can also try using your non-dominant hand to make the toss or do the trick using larger objects that require you to use both hands to catch it.

People will be more impressed with items other than balls and they are often easier to catch. A ball is more likely to bounce off your catching hand or back. Heavier objects, like a set of car keys, make for an impressive display and impacts your hand hard enough to make for an easy catch. This is not a trick you repeat, just slip it in occasionally. If you play sports, there may be times that a ball just happens to be in the proper position to catch it behind your back. Line it up for the catch and you might even impress yourself. Flawless with the trick? Try an egg and be eggceptional!

#33 Leaf It To Me

A simple trick that is a lot of fun involves grabbing a leaf, putting it into your almost closed hand and launching it into the air with a loud pop. Although the trick is not death-defying, it is guaranteed to produce a smile.

The key to the trick is bringing both of your hands together quickly in a position that trap the air. One hand is stationary while the other hand slaps it. If you wear a ring, remove it, or use the ring hand as your stationary hand. This will keep you from bruising your hand on the ring when you perform or practice the trick. Since practice requires repeated slapping, it may be prudent to limit your practicing attempts each day so that you avoid injury and becoming slap happy.

Close the fingers of your stationary hand and form a circle with your thumb and the end of your index finger. Leave at least a one-inch hole at the top of the hand as you will be eventually launching the leaf straight up into the air. Squeeze all your fingers together to prevent air from escaping between them. The bottom of the hand is more open than the top. Essentially, you have created a cavity of air.

Take the non-stationary hand and cup it slightly, squeezing your fingers together and pressing your thumb along the side of the palm and index finger. Place it next to your stationary hand and find the best position for them to fit together without allowing air to escape, except through the top of your stationary hand. Most will find that the perfect position will result in the thumb nail of your stationary hand being just behind the nail of your slapping hand. Strive to have the only hole at the top of your stationary hand when both hands meet. Keep the rest of the setup as tight as you can get it.

Slap the cupped hand hard into the stationary hand until you succeed in hearing a popping noise caused by the air rushing out. This is a simple trick so once you hear the popping noise, it is time to go outside and find a freshly fallen leaf or pull one off a tree. Tear the leaf into a circle or oval slightly larger than the top hole on your stationary hand. The size of the leaf is not overly critical. Have your stationary hand in its ready position and push the torn leaf into the top hole of your hand from the bottom up. The leaf should be cupped upwards and positioned to limit air gaps. Now that the stationary hand is loaded with the leaf, slap the hand hard, as you have been practicing. Done correctly, the leaf should fly about four feet into the air and the popping noise should be louder than when you practiced without the leaf.

When you demonstrate the trick, do it on a windless day. Allow your audience to see you carefully tearing the leaf and positioning it. It will make the feat look more challenging. Once they hear the theatrical pop, it is easy to go out on a limb and say that your audience will have a firm be-leaf in your skills.

#34 Roll Playing

Demonstrated in the movie <u>Illusionist</u>, this short trick shows your total control over a ball. The ball starts in your hand down by the side of the body and, as the ball is swung up past the body, climbs the fingers and ends up on the back of the hand. For a moment, the ball remains balanced on the back of the hand, until it is rolled off the fingers and back into the palm of your hand.

To learn the trick, pick a small ball about two and half inches in diameter. The trick can be done with larger balls of up to about six inches, but the smaller ball will look better. Select a ball that has a bit of weight to it. This is not a trick where you grab any ball and demonstrate your skill. Each ball will vary. A situation may occur where you could sneak out of view and practice a bit with an unfamiliar ball. Otherwise, use a ball that you are occasionally around, like a lacrosse or rubber dog ball. The web site has a suggested clear acrylic ball that looks mystifying.

There are two separate movements in this trick.

Practice them separately and then combine them once you have both down. Start the first movement with the ball in the palm of your hand. Have your arm down by your hip but twist your wrist so that your palm is facing out to the side. With your elbow slightly bent, swing your arm out and up in front of your face. Open your hand up allowing the ball's momentum to climb up your hand between the index finger and middle finger. The key to the trick is gauging the speed of your swinging arm. The ball, due to centrifugal force should approach the end of your fingertips just as your hand is pointing straight up. Allow the ball to roll over on to the back of your hand at this point. Control your arm's speed so that the ball never leaves contact with your hand.

Your hand should come to rest at chin height with its palm down. The ball should be motionless on the back of your hand resting between the tops of your index and middle fingers.

The second movement of the trick involves returning the balanced ball to the palm of your hand. Start with the ball balanced on the back of your hand between your index finger and middle finger in the position that you ended the first step.

Spread your index finger and middle finger to cause the ball to start rolling toward your fingertips. As soon as the ball starts rolling, slightly raise the back of your hand and your fingertips. As the ball is dropping between your index finger and middle finger, slightly squeeze the fingers together propelling it back toward the palm of your hand. Allow your thumb to catch the ball from below. Practice the two separate movements of the trick until they are smooth and then combine them.

As impressive as this looks, your demonstration only scratches the surface. Check out "contact juggling" or Fushigi and be prepared to be astonished. This is in the category of art and an artist like this can always draw a crowd!

#35 Drop the Subject

The Egg Drop is an easy trick where little skill is required other than collecting the supplies you need. In this trick, you stack a piece of cardboard, an empty toilet paper roll and an egg above a glass. As you hit the edge of the cardboard, the egg will drop into the glass. It is more of a physics demonstration, rather than a trick, but it has an element of danger that makes it enjoyable to watch. If you screw up, you will have to scramble to clean up a huge mess, possibly frying your friendship. On that note, practice the trick before you eat breakfast since the egg will probably get hairline cracks even as it successfully hits the water in the glass.

As with many other tricks in the book, you will be inspired to demonstrate the trick when you run across the particular props you need. There are five items you need for your demonstration, but the empty toilet paper roll is the hardest to collect. Although you could bring an empty toilet paper roll with you, the trick will look set up. It is better demonstrated impromptu. Grabbing an empty toilet paper roll or cutting down an empty paper towel roll is better.

With an empty toilet paper roll in hand, you will need the help of your host or the cook. Collect an egg, a tall glass and a piece of cardboard. Any unboiled egg will do. A tall glass, versus a short glass will make the egg's drop more dramatic plus it gives the egg a better chance of surviving the fall. The mouth or diameter of the glass should be about three inches to accommodate the falling egg. Hopefully, your host will have an empty box you can use but there are many cardboard items in a house. Even a nearly empty cereal box will do. The cardboard may be thin or thick and should be anywhere from seven to eleven inches long and at least five inches wide. Cut it down, if necessary. It is important to have at least an inch and a half of the cardboard cantilevered over the glass's edge.

Inevitably, guests will gather in the kitchen. Fortunately, that is the perfect spot to handle broken eggs and splashing water! Fill the water glass with three inches of water or more. The water will provide a cushion for the egg when it lands. Expect the egg to get some minor cracks. Balance the cardboard piece centered on top of the glass. Stack the toilet paper roll vertically on top of the cardboard, directly centered over the glass. Check your placement from at least two directions. Finally, balance the egg on its side or horizontally on top of the toilet paper roll.

Keep your audience's attention through this process and build suspense with the crowd. Make up a short story about how eggs influenced your ancestors in the 1800's or tell a fun fact about eggs. Did you know that a hen turns her eggs up to fifty times a day to keep the yolk from sticking to the sides?

Once the stage is set, hit the edge of the cardboard with a quick snap of your hand and wrist. Avoid hitting the glass with any follow through. The cardboard and toilet paper roll will fly out of the way, and gravity will take over. The egg should fall into the glass and make a splash, just like your trick!

#36 Recycle It

Flipping a water bottle was popularized by a viral video where Michael Senatore flipped a soft plastic water bottle at a high school talent show, landing it upright on a table. The crowd went wild! With a little bit of practice using good technique, you will be able to master this skill, as well.

The most important element of success in doing this trick is consistency. Try to keep the water level the same each time when you demonstrate the trick. Also, keep the way you grab the bottle and your swinging motion the same. Use the same brand of water bottle as the bottles vary a bit. Controlling your breath, heartbeat, perspiration rate and bottled up emotions might be taking it too far, but you get the drift.

Collect a half dozen empty water bottles before starting as they will be damaged as you practice. Fill all of them with about two inches of water. Most bottles have circular indentations around them that you can use as fill lines. After you start learning the

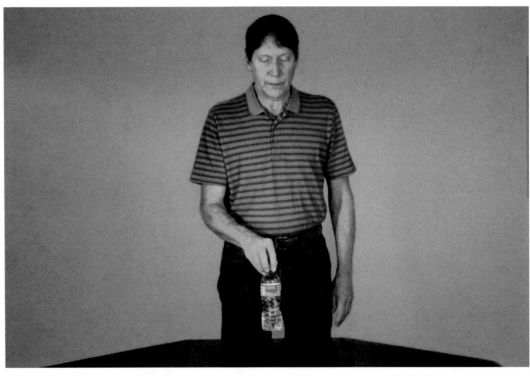

trick, experiment on how much water you want to have in the bottles. The level of water can vary from twenty to forty percent depending on your preference. It is not that critical if you are consistent with the amount used. Weight is important for flipping the bottle, but a heavier bottle seems to bounce more when it lands, so experiment.

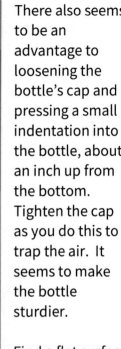

There also seems to be an advantage to loosening the bottle's cap and pressing a small indentation into the bottle, about an inch up from the bottom. Tighten the cap as you do this to trap the air. It seems to make the bottle sturdier.

Find a flat surface like a table or counter. Put the bottle on the table and grip the cap with all your fingers. This will allow for a consistent release of the bottle. If you hold the bottle in your hand to flip it, the bottle can fall to the side as well as front to back.

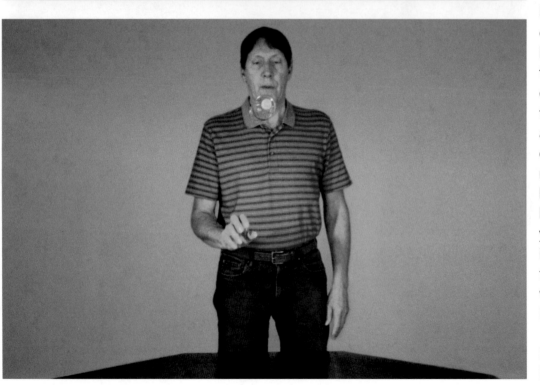

Pull the bottle back toward your

body, let the water settle, and swing the bottle up and out away from you as you flip it. If you are successful, the bottle will land on its base and stand upright. Missed attempts damage the flat bottom of the bottles, so replace the water bottles as needed when you are practicing. Develop muscle memory on how hard to swing the bottle and be fluid!

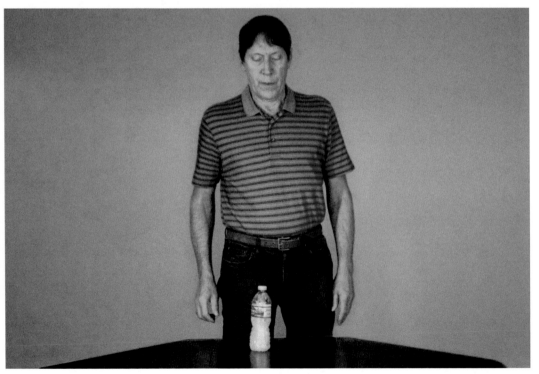

#37 Fake News

Among the easiest of the tricks is demonstrating a broken wrist. This trick will require some acting ability and proper timing. Once you practice the trick a few times you will be ready to approach a small group of people. Have your forearm outstretched with your "damaged" wrist supported by your other hand. Once you have everyone's attention, announce that you took a fall and think you broke your wrist. At this point you twist your wrist with the supporting hand and to the horror of the crowd, they hear a terrible sound. Some will think you have broken your wrist while others will laugh at your display. Either way, you will have some fun with it.

The cracking sound will be achieved by breaking a hard-plastic cup. You will need some plastic cups and a mirror to practice. Hard plastic cups crack into pieces and make the best noise. The web site has suggested plastic cups to buy.

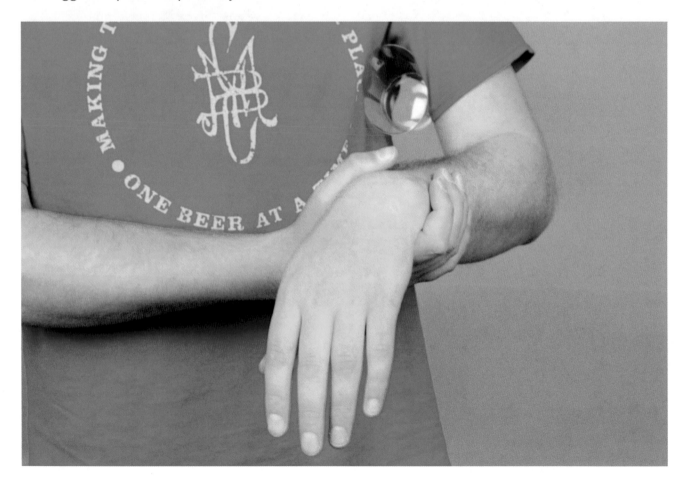

It is best to demonstrate your broken wrist with a layer of clothing between you and the plastic cup. The padding should keep you from being cut or scratched by the cup that you are breaking. An outer layer like a sweater or jacket will keep the cup from being seen. Place a plastic cup under your armpit, in between your shirt and the jacket, with the mouth of the cup facing forward. Lower your arm slowly on the cup until you feel it bend a bit, being careful not to break it. This will keep the cup secure until you are ready to twist your wrist. Practice walking around with the undamaged cup under your arm. Since you are holding the arm in a stationary position, it will be easy to do.

To hone your acting abilities and the timing of the demonstration, practice in front of a mirror. The hand on your "injured" limb should start palm down. Slide your supporting hand underneath the palm and twist the palm upwards. Through this process, keep your forearm stationary and just twist the wrist. Time twisting the wrist as you are squeezing your armpit and crunching the cup.

Set up the trick by going out of sight from the group, maybe to the restroom. Be organized enough to bring a cup or perform it at an event that is using hard plastic cups. Demonstrate the trick and wait for people's reactions. Then, announce that you do not find health related puns funny anymore since you now suffer from an irony deficiency.

#38 Spin Doctor

Most good basketball players can spin a basketball in the air and balance it on their finger. You do not need to play basketball to acquire this skill, but having a basketball is important. Although one can use almost any ball that has some weight, a basketball is perfect for learning this trick.

Grab a basketball with two hands on the lower half of the ball. Have one of your hands on the front side of the ball toward you, and the other hand either on the rear side of the ball away from you or on the bottom. Use your fingertips to hold the ball, not your palms. Rotate both of your hands either clockwise or counterclockwise as fast as you can, releasing the ball. The ball may be spun up in the air a foot or more but minimizing the launch of the ball to a few inches makes it easier. The ball should be spinning in the air, with the axis being as vertical as possible, meaning that the "equator" of the spinning ball is horizontal. Take advantage of the lines on the basketball to visually double check it. Otherwise, you will have trouble balancing the basketball on your finger.

As the basketball is spinning in the air, put your index finger under the axis. If you find that using your index finger is tough, try using your middle finger instead. Have your hand comfortably open at this point. Your palm should be facing you. This will allow you to make quick adjustments with your arm and wrist to keep the spinning ball balanced. The index or middle finger may be curved slightly and supported with the thumb or other fingers. The curved finger also allows you to balance the ball using your nail which has an advantage over using the end of your finger due to friction. Note: If your fingernails are too long, cut them before they get too out of hand.

If you are having trouble putting your finger under the axis of the ball, throw the ball up higher and follow it up with your index finger. This will help you to see the bottom of the ball and find the axis.

As you get the trick down, try using only one hand to spin the ball. Hold the ball in the fingertips of one hand and spin it with your wrist.

To dress up your new skill, use your fingers from your free hand to brush the side of the spinning ball to keep it spinning. Barely graze the side of the ball.

If you are terrific at spinning a basketball on your finger, try spinning a football. You will spin the ball the same way as the basketball but have the football's laces up. The ball should spin with the ends rotating the farthest distance. Find the exact axis point on the seam under the ball and mark it with a marker. This is where your finger needs to support the football, sew it seams!

#39 Holding All the Cards

L ook like a card shark with these two tricks. Both methods involve holding a deck of cards in one hand and moving the bottom half of the deck to the top. The tricks look a lot harder than they are.

Decks of cards come in two main sizes, the poker deck and the bridge deck. For those with smaller hands, try the bridge deck that is narrower. The web site has suggested decks to buy.

In the first method, grab the deck of cards and place it in your dominant hand. Adamantly support the deck at the center of the long sides between your thumb on one side, and the middle finger and ring finger on the other side. Allow your pinky to be on the end of the deck to keep the top cards from slipping off. Have the deck elevated above the palm of your hand with your curled index finger supporting the cards from below. The index fingernail is touching the deck. Slightly bend your thumb releasing the bottom half of the deck into the palm of your hand. Next, push the fallen portion of the

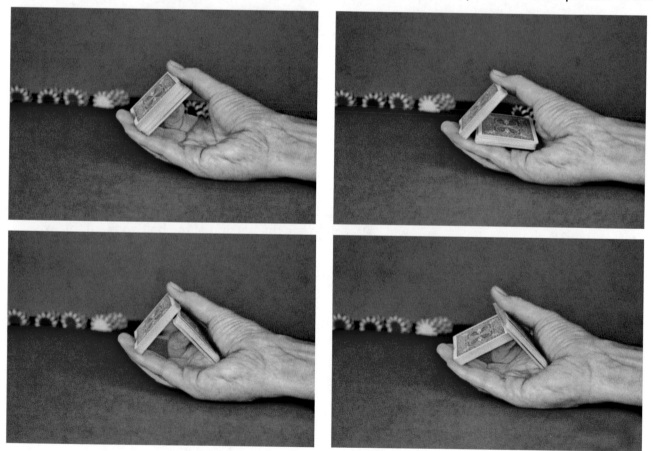

deck up with your index finger. The side of the bottom half of the deck slides along the bottom card of the upper half of the deck. Push until the bottom half of the deck forces your thumb out of the way, allowing the top half of the deck to fall into your index finger. As soon as that happens, get your index finger out of the way and close your hand around the full deck. For practice, use your other hand to reset the deck into the starting position and repeat. Eventually, use only one hand.

For the second method, grab the deck of cards with your dominant hand. As in the first method, the deck is elevated above the palm of your hand. This time support the deck from the long sides of the cards between your index finger and middle finger. Allow your thumb to slip toward your little finger around the corner of the deck. Use the inside

of your thumb to swing the top portion of the deck off causing it to rotate one hundred and eighty degrees. Start closing your hand, as you tuck the top half of the deck under the bottom half. For practice, use your other hand to reset the deck into the starting position and repeat.

Once you have both methods down, alternate the tricks back to back. Practice relying on just one hand. If you are not able to, it is not a big deal! Find comfort in the old adage, that three fingers were willing to cooperate, but the thumb and forefinger were opposed – or just practice more.

#40 Casting a Long Shadow

Occasionally, you might see a beam of light from a car, flashlight, movie projector or other source shining on a wall like a screen. If you can get between the source of the light and the screen, you can make the silhouette of an animal or what is called a shadow animal. This chapter will teach you how to make two shadow animals. Although you can try to do any animal, some are more recognizable and easier to create than others. These two animals check both boxes.

First, you will need a light source. A flashlight works well. Depending on its strength, you can even keep the lights on in the room. Turn on the flashlight, put it on the edge of a piece of furniture pointing the beam at a wall and pull up a chair to sit in.

A common and good shadow animal that many people demonstrate is the dog shadow. It is easy to learn. The dog shadow is done using one hand. Hold out your open hand vertically with your fingers together, perpendicular to the light source with your thumb up. It does not matter if your palm is facing the light source or facing away. Curl back your index finger while keeping the tip of the index finger touching your middle finger. This will allow a little bit of light to go between your index finger and middle finger creating the dog's eye and adding shape to the dog's head. If there is any light passing between your middle finger and ring finger, rotate your wrist slightly to eliminate it. The middle finger naturally sticks out a little farther than the ring finger making the dog's nose. If that is not the case with your hand, pull the ring finger back a touch. Next, use your thumb to make an ear. The little finger forms the dog's mouth and moves slowly up and down. Add a final touch, if you like, by making a whining or barking sound while moving the dog's mouth.

An elephant is created using two hands. The lower hand forms the trunk. Start out with your palm facing the floor and all your fingers next to each other. The beam of light should be hitting the side of your hand. While keeping your palm still, bend all four of your fingers pointing to the ground. Bend your wrist down, as well, to make the trunk longer. Have the middle and ring finger make the trunk. Divide these fingers ever so slightly to allow the end of the trunk to have a little indentation in it. If you have large hands, stick out just the little finger to make a tusk and leave the index finger next to the middle finger so that it is unused and hidden in the shadow. If you have small hands, you can stick out your little finger and the index finger for two great looking tusks as the tusks look better thin. The thumb is tucked up next to the side of the hand and the tip dropped very slightly to make a small mouth.

Now, get the upper hand on the trick! The upper hand is used to create the head of the elephant. Mimic the general shape of the lower hand with its palm down, and the same finger and wrist bend. Place the upper hand with the side of your index finger next to the largest knuckle on your lower hand. Look at the shadow and allow your upper hand to be a continuation of the silhouette of the elephant's head. The top of your thumb rests against the lower hand, too. Keep the hands together with a little pressure, making them one unit. Create the elephant's eye by allowing a trace of light to go through the area between the thumb and the hand. Learn to adjust your two wrists and forearms so that no light, other than that for the eye, comes through on the elephant's head and that the elephant's neck looks normal. As a final touch, wiggle the trunk slowly and if you like, add the trumpeting sound that elephant's make.

With both shadow animals, stick only the portion of the animal that you want people to see into the light source. With the elephant, you can create a bit of the back of the elephant without showing the front legs that you are unable to make.

Practicing for several sessions will perfect your technique and your animal magnetism. Warning: It is a fact that if your flashlight batteries die, you will be delighted.

#41 Twirligig

This demonstration involves twirling an umbrella, cane, stick, pool cue, golf club, lacrosse stick or any other item that is long and slender. Once you learn this trick, you will be able to do it with all the above. The trick is quite easy to do and fun.

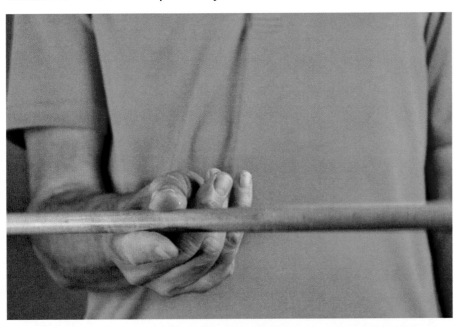

Since objects like an umbrella, a cane or a golf club are off balanced, initially practice by grabbing an easier item that has its center of gravity in the middle. The middle point on the item should have equal weight on both sides. Grab something like a four-foot-long, three-quarter inch doweling. If you have some brooms or rakes at home, unscrew the handle from the head. The center of gravity should be the center of the stick.

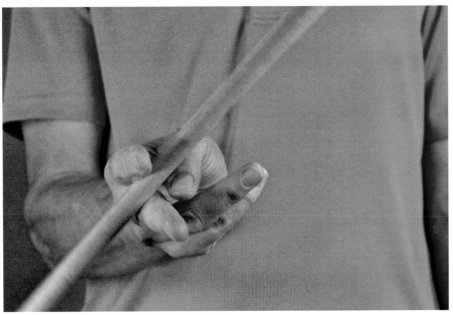

With your palm up, place the center of the stick into your hand as if you were holding a big pencil or pen. The thumb and index finger are holding the stick while your middle finger helps support the weight. If you are using your right hand, you will be twirling the stick counterclockwise, whereas the left hand will be clockwise. If you are using your right hand, it will benefit you to have the left

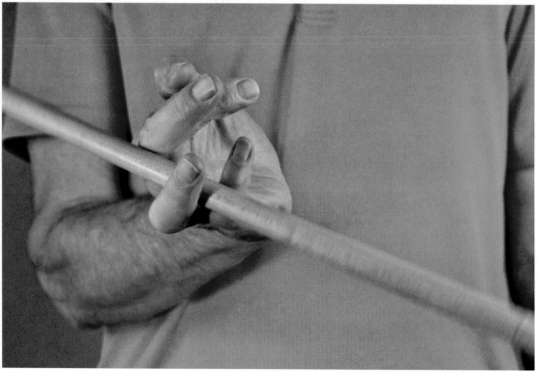

end of the stick higher than the right end to give some momentum to begin the twirl. While keeping your palm up or at a forty-five-degree angle, twist your wrist slightly and release your thumb's hold on the stick. The stick should start spinning to where it is first being held between your index finger and your middle finger, then between the middle finger and the ring finger, and finally between the ring finger and the little finger. To make this possible, you will need to have the trailing fingers pulled in

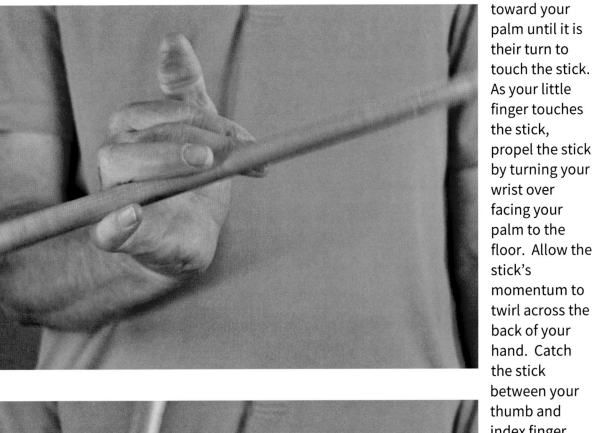

toward your palm until it is their turn to touch the stick. As your little finger touches the stick, propel the stick by turning your wrist over facing your palm to the floor. Allow the stick's momentum to twirl across the back of your hand. Catch the stick between your thumb and index finger wrapping your hand around it.

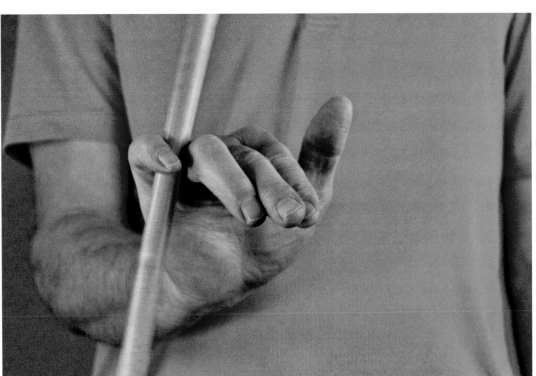

Once you get this down, practice with items that are off balanced. Grab the object at its balancing point, or close by. Guess where the balancing point is and double check by placing the

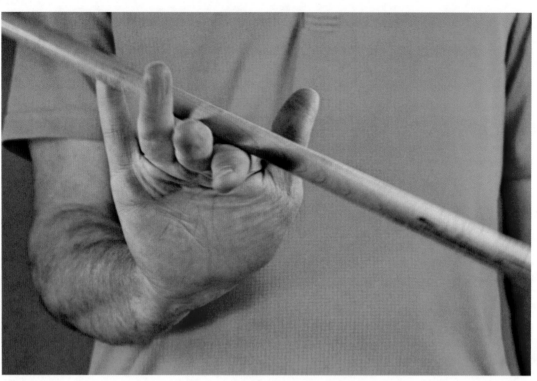

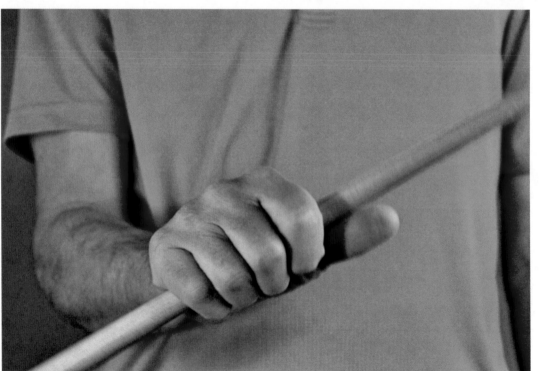

item horizontally on an outstretched finger to see where it balances. Realize that if you grab a cane or a golf club, the weight of the handle or club head will shift its balancing point toward the heavy end by up to eight inches or more. With a little practice, you will be ready for any item you run across.

The umbrella presents a different challenge as the material makes it thick and harder to twirl, but it also makes for a mist defying display!

#42 Kickback

It takes real commitment and serious training to be good at soccer, but this is a trick that most soccer players do that will impress everyone. The soccer ball is rolled up the inside of your calf, pushed out toward your backside, kicked up in the air and caught.

Although this trick is more physically challenging than most of the tricks in the book, you are just making a hop and one kick. Even nonathletes will see progress after an hour or so of practice. Practice for ten minutes at a time and stop when you do as well or better than the last practice. End on a good note! If you have any doubt on whether you are healthy enough to practice this trick, please check with your physician.

Although you have a dominant and nondominant hand, many people do not think of their legs in the same way. Each leg will have a different job to do in this trick. Initially, experiment switching the roles of both feet. One combination will be easier for you. Once you find it, stick with that combination.

The best place to practice the trick is outside. Soccer balls can do damage!

While standing, trap the soccer ball between your feet. Lift one of your feet, rolling the ball up and down the inside of the opposite calf. Repeat this action and get used to this move with your launching foot. Once you feel comfortable doing this, aggressively roll the ball up the inside of your calf and release it toward your backside, forcing the ball to pop up a foot or two. Use your other foot, the kicking foot, to kick the ball up in the air with the heal or inside of the foot. As the launching foot is in the air, the kicking foot needs to hop to kick the soccer ball as you are airborne. The kicking foot must reach back behind the launching foot to kick the ball. Look over your shoulder so that you have a chance to make the proper contact. Most find that jumping forward a bit makes the trick easier. With practice you will learn to kick the ball out in front of you.

Soccer player's techniques vary widely. Find what allows you to do the trick consistently and use it. The ball can be kicked around the side of the launching leg or up and over the shoulder. The ball can be kicked really high or just barely clear your shoulders. Initially, turn your torso partially to catch the ball. Eventually you should not have to turn. In soccer, you need to be goal-oriented.

A great philosopher once said: Wearing tight jeans will make it hard to pull off.

#43 Accomplish-mint

Instead of simply placing a mint in your mouth, this trick involves launching a mint or other small food item off your open hand into your mouth. For training purposes, use mints. Pick an inexpensive brand of mints like Tic Tac's that gives you multiple unwrapped mints in a little container. Warning! A dropped mint may not be in mint condition!

In general, since you are launching a food item or mint at your mouth with some force, pick an item that will not crack a tooth or cause an eye injury. As another precaution, when you open your mouth wide, do not expose the front of your teeth. Also, if you are going to learn this trick, understand that there is always the risk of choking whenever food is involved. This is especially true of this trick as you are catching food toward the back of your throat. Do not practice the trick without supervision.

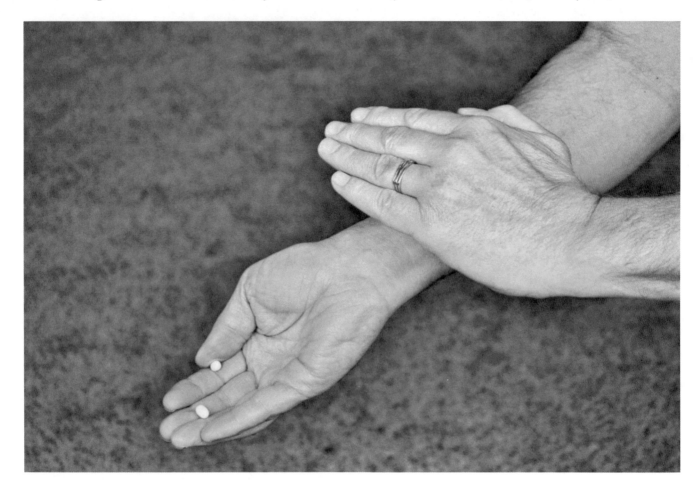

Hold your hand palm up with your fingers together at about chest height. The hand should be directly in front of your body with your fingers pointing away from you. Have your fingers pointing either straight away from you or up at a slight angle. Initially, your wrist should be about six inches from your mouth to make it easier. With practice you can lengthen this distance to about a foot. Put a mint into your cupped fingers and open your mouth wide. Simultaneously, move the hand holding the mint toward your mouth while using the tips of the fingers on your other hand to slap down on the area where the heel of the hand meets your wrist. This will turn your hand into a catapult launching the mint toward your mouth. Slap the heel more than the wrist as the heel is tougher and can sustain the blows better. Keep your eye on the mint. With practice you should be able to hit your mouth consistently. As you do, lengthen the distance you propel the mint. You should also practice the trick from a standing and sitting position. People will be impressed with even the shorter distances, especially if they try to duplicate the trick.

If you find this trick easy, try doing it with two mints back to back. Hold the first mint to be launched in the usual spot. The second mint is pinned down by your thumb but visible to viewers. After you launch the first mint, use your thumb to release and push the second mint into your cupped fingers, and launch it. Really, the decision to do one mint or two is a toss-up.

#44 Penmanship

This is among the harder tricks in the book. Since most of us are around pens and pencils daily, one has great flexibility on when to use the trick. The trick involves holding a pen and spinning it. It can be repeated many times, but it is not a trick you want to call attention to. Rather, use it subtly in a classroom or a board meeting. If you tend to fidget, twirl your pen when you are all alone.

For training, use the writing instrument you use daily. Throughout your practice, the hand itself needs to remain still. There is no twisting or bouncing. Some may find that resting the forearm on the edge of a table will help. All the pen's motion is caused by the middle finger. Start by holding your pen in your writing hand as if you were going to write something. However, it is important to hold the pen closer to the top as you want the end of the pen with the tip to weigh more. Next, shift the middle finger so that the finger is resting on the outside of the pen, away from you. You will find that you will

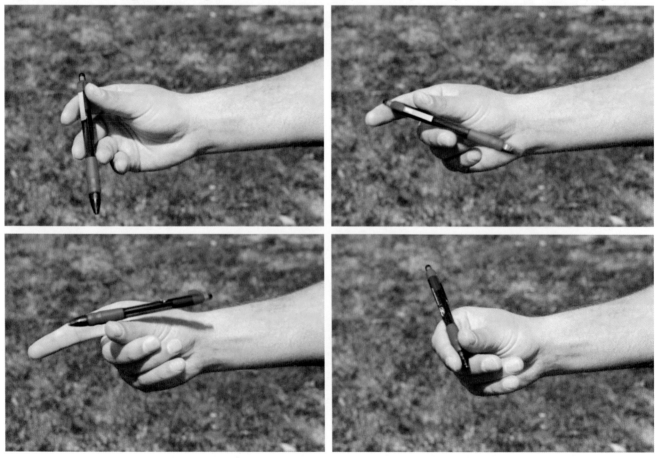

need to slightly tighten the grip of your index finger and thumb to keep it from falling into your ring finger. Apply just enough pressure to keep the pen from falling.

Flick your middle finger back toward your palm pushing the pen into a spin. The goal is to have the pen swing up over your thumb and come to rest in the "V" created by your thumb and index finger, allowing you to start writing with the pen. Experiment to find the proper speed that you must propel the pen. For better consistency, try to spin the pen on a vertical rather than a flat plane.

As a practicing tip, count the number of attempts you need to make to succeed in doing the trick and write it down. This will encourage you. It may take you two hundred tries to do the trick for the first time, a hundred tries the second time, fifty tries the third and fifteen tries the fourth. It is the sort of trick that once you are consistent, you will wonder why it took you so long to learn it.

Once you become de-pen-dable with the trick and can draw attention to yourself, any writing instrument will do. Then you can apply the techniques learned to a spoon, drumstick or other long objects.

#45 Driver's Ed

This trick is easy to demonstrate when you are on the tee box preparing to tee off. In this case, you will trap the golf ball between your foot and the head of the driver, pop the ball up, then use the top of the driver to launch the ball up into the air and catch it.

To practice, grab a golf ball, your wedge and your driver. Wear the shoes you play golf in. Initially, learn the launching part of the trick utilizing your wedge because it is an easier club to work with. Put the golf ball down on any low-cut grassy area similar to a tee box. Grab your wedge with your dominant hand and place the opposite foot next to the golf ball so that the ball is on the inside of your foot. The golf ball may be near the ball of your foot or more toward your instep or arch. Place the front edge of your wedge next to the golf ball wedging it (no pun intended), between the golf club and your shoe. Lift both your foot and the club simultaneously trapping the ball enough to pop the ball into the air. Pop the golf ball up about a foot then use your club's face to tap the ball up in the air and catch it. Throughout the process, your knee does not come straight up, but rather is lifted to the side a bit away from your body. Once lifted, you should be looking down at the inside of your shoe.

The wedge is an easy club to use to pop up the ball because the face is very open. Once you have the motion down with the wedge and foot, try popping up the ball with the driver. The driver has a very flat club face making the initial trap and launch more difficult. Since the driver is a longer club, grab it a little lower on the grip for more control. Remember to trap the ball and lift both your foot and the driver simultaneously. As you launch the ball, be prepared to use the top of the club head, not the face, to tap the ball up in the air to catch it. It is common for the top of the driver to be rounded. Concentrate on making contact on the inside portion of the club head nearest you so that the ball bounces toward your hand.

As with many other tricks in the book, only demonstrate the trick on the tee box once or twice during your round of golf. Overusing your skill will diminish its impressiveness. Time this trick to when the rest of your foursome has their attention on their preparation. Leave them impressed as they catch a glimpse of the trick. They will develop a driving ambition to duplicate it.

#46 The Tipping Point

One of the simplest tricks in the book is balancing a soda can at an angle on its bottom edge. Although it looks like a magic trick as the soda can mysteriously balances, it is very simple science. Most people have seen the trick but will enjoy seeing it again.

Just a little practice is necessary. Since beer and pop cans vary a bit, grab an empty one of the brand you usually drink. Fill it with water anywhere between one and two inches. The typical aluminum can have a tapered edge that runs from the bottom of the can to the side of the can at an angle. Place the can on its bottom edge and slowly release your grip. As you barely release your grip, you should be able to tell that the can is balancing and does not need your support. In practice, experiment a little with the level of water needed. Being consistent with the water level later is the only skill you need to develop.

Since everyone can replicate the trick, pick your time to demonstrate the trick wisely to get the most mileage out of it. Wait till your group is interacting so you do not have to draw attention to this modest trick. Also, make sure the table is stable as someone could bump into it causing a spill. Kitchen islands work well, are very stable and usually collect a crowd at a party.

When you are ready to demonstrate the trick, drink your beverage down to the estimated range and do your balancing act. If you are even slightly worried about the level of liquid, subtly test balance the can out of view or wait until people are distracted. If it falls during your demonstration, it would be soda pressing!

#47 The Photo Op

This is a fun trick where you take a picture of a person and tell them about a new app on your phone. This app can amazingly remove a person from a picture. After moving your finger a few times on your phone's screen, you show the person that they have been removed from the photo you just took.

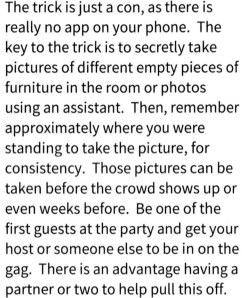

The trick is just a con, as there is really no app on your phone. The key to the trick is to secretly take pictures of different empty pieces of furniture in the room or photos using an assistant. Then, remember approximately where you were standing to take the picture, for consistency. Those pictures can be taken before the crowd shows up or even weeks before. Be one of the first guests at the party and get your host or someone else to be in on the gag. There is an advantage having a partner or two to help pull this off.

Wait until the party starts and take a picture of a person sitting in a chair or a group sitting on a couch. As you are scrolling through your phone to find the picture you took earlier, excitedly tell them about the app you just downloaded and show them the altered picture. Have your well instructed partner standing by watching. Your "subjects" will either be astonished, or they just will not believe it. Regardless, have your assistant state that you demonstrated the app to him earlier and that the app is really amazing. At this time, one of you should suggest you take another picture of the disbeliever. Have your accomplice set up the second picture as they know which side of the person to be on and where the picture should be taken. The background needs to match the picture you took earlier. As the photographer, you should be adjusting yourself into the position you need to be shooting from, as well. Repeat the trick using the pictures you took earlier of your collaborator or empty furniture. Those initial pictures should have your assistant posing in several different positions like an arm over the shoulders, an arm around the waist or even kissing the cheek of the "erased" person. Always let your subjects in on the gag and share a laugh. Prolonging the joke might embarrass them.

Although the example used above is in a person's house, think creatively. Demonstrate your "app" any time you can predict where someone will be. The person might be at a playground, swimming up to the side of the pool to speak to you, fishing in their favorite spot, sitting on the bench in a park or leaning against their car waiting for you. People are creatures of habit.

If you have several people meeting in a cafeteria or restaurant and you know that everyone is dragging in individually, you have the perfect scenario. Be the first one there so you can take the initial picture of the empty table. Pull this joke on the first couple people who show up and let them in on the con, making them co-conspirators. Conveniently, you caught the picture you need of them smiling for the next person that shows up, as their relative position at the table has not changed. Instead of showing the picture of the empty table, you show the last picture you took of everyone but your new mark. Just con-tinue the trick taking a new picture every time someone shows up. Relax, you will not get arrested for indecent exposures!

#48 Backhanded

One of the more impressive tricks in this book is the act of flipping a coin across the back of your fingers. Although it is among the harder tricks in the book, you are guaranteed to impress all who see your skill.

Since hands come in different sizes, grab a selection of different sized coins. You might find coins from other countries to select from, as well. Most adults will find a larger coin, like a quarter, half dollar or dollar works well. Experiment with different size coins as you are working on the trick. Pick a location like lying in a bed, leaning back on a couch or sitting at a table to practice the trick. It will save you time picking up the dropped coin over and over!

Looking at the back of your fingers, you will utilize the area between the largest knuckles on the back of your hand and the next joint more toward the midpoint of your fingers. Hold your hand palm down

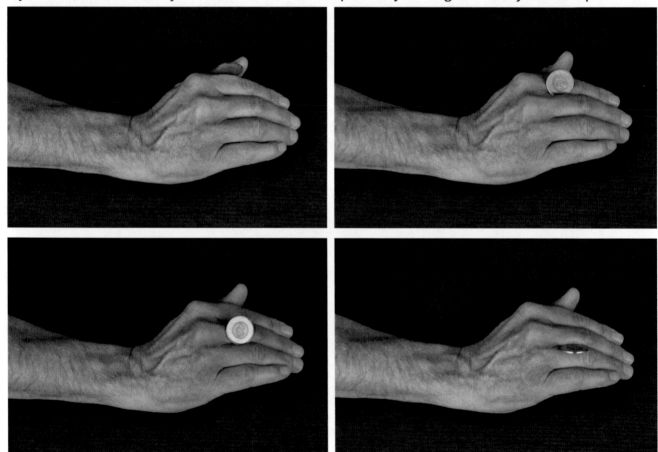

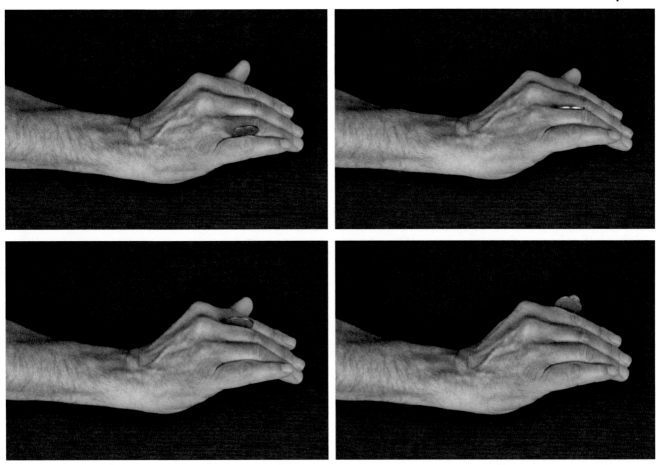

with your fingers extended and relaxed. Pinch the bottom edge of the coin between your thumb and the side of your index finger. Gently tilt the back of your fingers toward your little finger and release the coin with your thumb. This allows gravity to help. The coin should roll over the index finger and slide down into the crevice touching the middle finger. Keep your fingers close together so that the coin never falls through the crack between your fingers. As the coin travels down finger to finger, the receiving finger is always raised a little to catch the coin. Once stopped by the receiving finger, the sending finger is raised as the receiving finger is now lowered to flip the coin toward the next finger. You essentially create a wave motion with your fingers. Repeat this until the coin is raised vertically by the little finger. Tilt the hand back toward the thumb and the process of flipping the coin is reversed back through the fingers the opposite way. On the way back, when you flip the coin over the index finger, use your thumb to press on the edge of the coin raising it vertically on its end. Repeat the process of flipping the coin down and back a couple times, then end the trick. To end the trick, instead of having your thumb trap the coin, have it pull the coin into the palm of your hand.

As you get better at this trick, reevaluate the size of the coin you are using. With the proper coin and some practice, the coin should easily cascade across your fingers due to gravity, just like a Slinky goes down steps. Be prepared to quickly react to keep from dropping the fast-moving coin, when this happens, and end the trick on a high note.

Sharpen your skills by practicing the trick without looking. Not only will onlookers be amazed, but it will sharpen your control of the coin by touch. Consider this as free tech knuckle support.

#49 Put a Spin On It

One of the harder tricks in the book is spinning a tray on one finger. Unlike spinning a basketball on your finger, a tray just will not spin on a balance point for long. Where the basketball has gyroscopic tendencies, the tray does not.

If you are an adult, use a round sixteen-inch pizza tray with perforated holes for training. If you are younger, use a smaller, similar pizza tray. Initially, it is helpful to learn on an item that has some

weight and good traction on the bottom - in this case the holes in the pizza tray. The web site has a suggested pizza tray to buy. Once you learn the trick, your new skills can be applied to a variety of items. The objects will not need anything for traction, and they can even be rectangular, like a clipboard.

Take your tray and run a piece of one-inch wide colored tape from the center to the edge on the top of the pizza pan. The color contrast helps you see the tape, while the tray is spinning. This visual aid is helpful for training, but once you get the motion and timing down, the tape is unnecessary.

Rest assured, the tray will be dropped many times during practice, so practice over a bed or couch to cushion its fall and make the retrieval easy.

Start with the tray about chest height with your dominant hand under the tray. Use your other hand to support the tray from the far edge and to give the initial spin. Hold the tray with the strip of blue tape parallel to your body and pointing to the outside. The dominant hand should have its palm up with its middle finger placed under the tape about an inch off the center of the tray. Once you learn the trick, you will be able to use your ring finger or index finger, as well.

Pull the hand on the edge toward you, spinning the tray at a medium speed and release it. Try keeping the supporting finger under the piece of tape and match every revolution of the tray, using a circular motion with your hand and arm. Once you can spin the tray for three to five seconds, you will feel the timing necessary to advance your skills. Learning this skill is all about touch.

Understand that the farther off center your supporting finger is, the farther it must travel to complete the circle and the quicker your finger needs to move. If the finger is closer to the center, it will move slower. To keep the tray spinning, you will constantly be adjusting your speed. If you go too slow, the tray will wobble. Go too fast and the tray will fly off your finger.

It is important to spin the tray at a slight angle, not flat, tipped toward the spinning hand. Thus, the circular motion of your supporting finger is not flat either, but at an angle. Add a little power to the spinning tray every time it is going uphill to keep the momentum. The tray is trying to fall away from you, so if you impart the power on the downhill portion of the circular motion, the tray will want to fly off your finger. So, sling the tray a little on every upstroke. Mentally, on every rotation it helps to think, "sling it up", "sling it up", etc. As you improve with this trick, you will adjust to each item you spin since they will feel different on your finger. You will spin larger objects slower and smaller objects faster. When you switch to an object like a clipboard, the center point will not be the balancing point due to the weight of the metal end. Find the balancing point by shifting your starting position slightly toward the metal side of the clipboard. This is a hard trick so remember, if at first you don't succeed, tray, tray again!

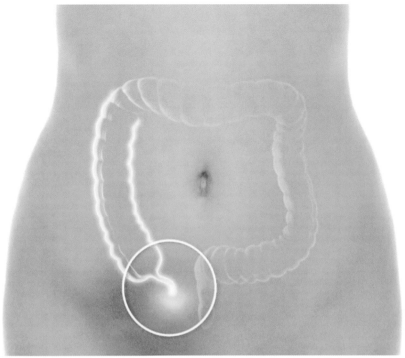

Appendix photo by Shutterstock.com

As a reader of this book, you clearly appreciate learning new things and bettering your life. The goal of this book is to positively affect the lives of our readers. Being a little cooler just might help the start of a romance, set you up for a job promotion, improve your confidence and more.

In the spirit of self-improvement, we offer you this used appendix. The information here is not a new concept. Similar things have been recommended by many in the past. The following exercises can provide you with a road map toward having a great life and career. You have the choice of waking up each morning and allowing life to pull you along and be average, or you can choose to be the captain of your own ship. We suggest you make a plan and follow the plan. Finish each day knowing that you are a step closer to achieving your goals.

Successful people tend to be organized and make lists. The following exercises involve you making your own lists. They should be personal and private, like a diary. Using your computer will be the most efficient, but you may find a journal more satisfying.

In the first exercise, write down a list of personal statements of who you are and who you aspire to be as a person. Write them in first person to program your mind when you read them and try to read them often. There is an actual benefit to reading them out loud. Here are some good examples, but they will be more meaningful if you write your own:

- I treat my family as if they are my most valued possession.
- Every day I strive to become more effective and functional.
- I handle crowds and audiences with ease because I am confident.
- I am warm, friendly and well-liked.
- I face each day confident in my ability to handle the details of my thoughts and actions.
- I try to be humble and treat others with kindness.
- I remember to thank God for his blessings and talk to him often.

The second exercise is creating a list of goals you would like to achieve in your lifetime. Cover both your personal and work life. Pick realistic goals. If you are 55 years old, it would be unusually difficult to compete in the Olympics. (Although Oscar Swahn of Sweden was 72 years old when he competed in shooting in the 1920 Olympics!) Pick goals that are achievable but aim high. Focus on these goals and even if you fall a bit short, you will have a life to be proud of. Here are some examples:

I want to…

- become an accomplished engineer, designing the largest bridges in the world.
- fall in love with the right person and do a great job as a parent.
- learn to fly.
- become a master electrician and own my own business.
- be healthy.
- start a non-profit to fund research to end blindness.
- own a big house on a lake.
- travel into space.
- compete in a triathlon.
- research ways to miniaturize good power sources.
- see the world.
- positively impact millions of people.

Your third exercise is to take each of your goals and write down all the steps necessary to achieve that goal. Break down each goal into subgoals that you work toward. Determine what skills, education, and money are required, and how you will get them. For instance, if you want to be a doctor, go on-line and research the steps required to become a doctor. You will find lots of advice, including items like taking particular tests and applying for a residency. Develop your personal list and expand it as much as you can. A subgoal to becoming a doctor may entail getting good grades, reading multiple anatomy books, learning a second language or eventually picking the right field to specialize in.

Depending on the goal, you might have five steps to get there, or you might have fifty steps. Some goals may be difficult and could take you many years to achieve them. Setting up a timetable to reach each of your subgoals creates a sense of urgency and commitment. Completing each subgoal will give you a feeling of accomplishment as you are one step closer to your goal. As you zero in on your goal, it becomes easier to put in the effort with the end in sight. Do not hesitate to seek great mentors along the way so that you move efficiently. Finding people that want to support you on your quest is easy if they know you are serious. Chart your path wisely.

As your life changes, you will need to review and revise your goals. A great opportunity may present itself or something new may catch your interest. Your last list should be the one that contains all the goals you achieve. Nothing is more satisfying than transferring a completed goal to your list of accomplishments. Look at that list often to remind yourself how awesome you are.

Build yourself a great life!

The End???

Be sure to subscribe to THAT'S COOL on YouTube.

See our video on this book along with training videos covering many other cool skills. Visit our website at:
https://www.thatscool.cool

Both sites have links to recommended products.

Made in the USA
Coppell, TX
19 December 2020